The Frugal Duchess

How to Live Well and Save Money

The Frugal Duchess

How to Live Well and Save Money

Sharon Harvey Rosenberg

The Frugal Duchess of South Beach

DPL
PRESS

Los Angeles

The Frugal Duchess: How to Live Well and Save Money

PRINTED IN THE UNITED STATES OF AMERICA

This book is designed to provide accurate and authoritative information on the subject of household and personal money management. It is sold with the understanding that neither the author nor the publisher are engaged in rendering legal, accounting, or other professional services by publishing this book. As each individual situation is unique, questions relevant to and specific to the individual should be addressed to an appropriate professional to ensure that the situation has been evaluated carefully and appropriately. Neither the author nor publisher represent in any way the viability or accuracy of anything offered herein. The author and publisher specifically disclaim any liability, loss, or risk that is incurred as a consequence, directly or indirectly, of the use and application of any of the contents of this work.

Cover Design: Jeremy Hunt, *www.SDMFX.com*

Cover Illustration: Joel Barbee, *www.JoelBarbee.com*

Author Photo: Melanie Bell

"Anti-Binge Strategies" on page 36 is reprinted with permission from *Woman's Day* magazine, September 2006, "The Tag Says $50, So What Will it Really Cost You?" by Mary Hunt.

"Are You a Compulsive Shopper?" pop quiz on page 36 is reprinted with permission from *Overcoming Overspending: A Winning Plan for Spenders and Their Partners,* by Olivia Mellan, psychotherapist, money coach (Walker & Company, 1997).

For information regarding special discounts for bulk purchases and or corporate branding, please contact:

DPL Press, Inc., P.O. Box 2135, Los Angeles, CA 90723;
Special Sales: 800-550-3502. Visit us at *DPLPress.com.*

Library of Congress Cataloging-in-Publication Data
Information Available by Request from Publisher

ISBN: 978-19345080-0-8

1   2   3   4   5   6   7   8   9   10

To M&D: Barbara and Ben Harvey

Thanks for teaching us how to dream,
save and live.

With love, from Sharon

Table of Contents

Introduction

I found my Dream House at a yard sale on Surprise Lake, a Miami Beach neighborhood that shares its name with a body of water that feeds into the Atlantic Ocean. The house—a two-story Mediterranean structure with a double lot backyard—was a good bargain, especially given the location: just 30 blocks north of South Beach, an international playground filled with trendy boutiques, nightclubs and cafes.

South Beach's all-night party crowd of supermodels, celebrities and drag queens was just going to sleep when I first toured that Dream House on a Sunday morning in the mid-1990s.

The homeowners were grandparents who were ready to move into a smaller home after many happy years in their 3,600-square-foot

Mediterranean home. My husband, Avi, and I—then young parents with pre-schoolers—chatted with the sellers, discovered a few mutual connections and looked over the yard sale merchandise. For just a few dollars, we purchased terracotta plant containers and several potted plants, including a robust aloe.

I was pleased with our purchases. Such yard sale expeditions are part of my thrifty-but-luxurious life, and my bargain-hunting experiences have provided plenty of material for my *Miami Herald* newspaper column and blog posts, where I am Sharon Harvey Rosenberg, aka "The Frugal Duchess." But as a bargain hunter, I missed the deal of the decade at that yard sale.

In hindsight, my husband and I should have skipped the plants and bought the yard. The asking price—about $425,000—was too rich for our budget, but we should have begged, borrowed, and saved to buy that house. That's because at $425,000, the Dream House was really a Dream Investment. Consider how the house has sold since that yard sale:

June 2000:	$675,000 Sold
June 2005:	$1.32 million Sold
November 2006:	$2 million Sold
March 2007:	$2.6 million Listed Sale Price

Clearly, we missed a great opportunity in the red-hot South Beach housing market. And it's not just a Miami thing. Double-digit gains in home prices from the mid-1990s through 2006 have locked many consumers—teachers, health care workers, police officers and store clerks—out of the home market or prompted home buyers to borrow far more than they can comfortably afford.

And while consumer debt has spiked to an all-time high, the rate of personal savings has dropped to the lowest levels since 1933. The financial crunch has been felt by consumers from the Gen Y set—ages 25 to 34—to baby boomers, ages 50 and up.

In my neighborhood, one older baby boomer uses the term "Splitting the Penny," to describe the challenge of taking care of day-to-day family expenses, while trying to save for long-term goals such as retirement and college educations for children and grandchildren. These days, I've been splitting a lot of pennies as I save for my $2.6 million Dream House, while maintaining a thrifty but upscale lifestyle on Miami Beach. I know that if I keep saving, I'll buy that yard sale house one day. Saving runs in my genes.

I come from generations of hard-working homeowners and big-time savers. Over the years, I've watched as my M&D worked extra jobs and saved for a series of successively larger homes, including a large ocean-front condo in Central Florida—all while sending four children to college. What's more, my great aunts, uncles, cousins and grandparents have owned property from the Deep South to the Northeast region of the United States. And through thrifty living, my younger siblings own homes in Pittsburgh, Washington, D.C., and Orlando.

We're a family of homeowners

So why is an economy-sized writer like me living in an ocean-view apartment in a big-ticket neighborhood filled with mansions, South Beach celebrities and late model cars? Quite simply, I'm taking frugal lessons from The (South Beach) Millionaire(s) Next Door. And the authors of that bestselling book about the thrifty habits of millionaires are right: Many—albeit clearly not all—of the wealthy are well-schooled in the art of luxury living for less. My life in the palm tree shade of wealth and privilege has taught me to buy designer clothes at thrift store prices, organic produce through a discount food co-op and to vacation at top-ranked resorts at budget-motel prices.

These frugal lessons continue the financial education I acquired in my parents' home, where fabulous living on a thrifty budget was the family code. In her spirit of "anything is possible," my mother smiles encouragingly when she hears me talk about my Dream House. Her advice: work, save and pray.

And indeed, my Mediterranean Mansion represents many things: my prayers, my financial strategies, my greatest disappointments and my highest aspirations. This is the story about what my Dream House— and other homes—have taught me about fine living, finance and faith. Each chapter includes the lessons I've learned and the mistakes I've made, with frugal tips from fellow bloggers in cyberspace. ☝

The View from My Porch

Almost every day from my "porch" (actually, it's the seventh-floor balcony) of my apartment, I study the object of my affection. It's like high school all over again. But instead of crushing on the cutest boy in my chemistry class, I am crushing on a tall Mediterranean with a clay tile roof. I love that house.

From my balcony I actually see very little of my big Dream House on the corner. The property is surrounded by a concrete wall, dense bushes and palm trees that shield the 11,000-square-foot lot from prying eyes.

What I can see from my balcony is a broad view of the Atlantic Ocean. Sitting on a cast-iron chair—a hand-me-down from my friend Caroline—I watch storm clouds dance over South Beach; I trace the skyline of famous Miami Beach hotels. Late in the afternoon, I follow the progress of large cruise ships en route to Caribbean ports. Clearly, I live in paradise.

As I relax on the porch with a homemade café latte or a tall glass of mint tea—cheaper and tastier than the Starbucks version—I feel so Southern. And living in Miami, I am truly in one of the most Southern points in the continental U.S. After living all over the Northeastern seaboard, I've finally come back home to the South.

My family tree is rooted in the South, where towns like Macon, Georgia, and King George, Virginia, are part of our family folk tales. As the descendents of slaves and sharecroppers, our lives are anchored to the South like an old land deed.

In my childhood, the South was as vivid as a mural on the wall or the mobile dangling over my crib. It was also the summer breeze from an open window, lifting and playing in the yellow eyelet curtains that hung in the kitchen. You couldn't see it and you couldn't touch it, but the South—the Good, the Bad and the Ugly—is our family ghost.

I've carried the South around in my luggage during my travels as a young urban professional. You could track my life and career by following the Amtrak route of the East Coast: Philadelphia, D.C., Pittsburgh, New York and, finally, Miami. And like a railroad drifter, I've had several jobs: television producer, shoe model, waitress, fact checker, financial writer, celebrity "stalker," magazine and newspaper columnist, and personal finance blogger.

The nomadic life of a journalist has taken a heavy toll on my finances. Obsessed with meeting deadlines and acquiring prestigious bylines, I often neglected my financial health.

How bad have I been? Consider a past battle between my dirty laundry and a pressing deadline.

Faced with a lack of time and a lack of clean clothes, I once took a very expensive route. Why waste hours and hours in a coin-operated laundry room, when I could buy ready-to-wear replacements in less time? That's what I did one day when I was in my early 20s. And in an Olympic-caliber performance, I jumped over my clothes hamper as if it were a mere hurdle in a race and sprinted to purchase a new wardrobe, designed to last until I had the time and energy to face my dirty clothes. Here's the score card:

Dirty Laundry vs. New Clothes		
Option	**Time**	**Cost**
Laundry	4 Hours	$4 (plus detergent)
New Wardrobe	30 Minutes	$150 (low-ball estimate)

I justified the mini-shopping spree—which I could not afford—by telling myself a series of lies and half-truths about my behavior and motives:

Top 10 Lies I Tell Myself

1. This purchase will pay for itself.

2. Sometimes, girl, you have to spend money to save money.

3. I'll work overtime to pay for it.

4. I'll save double next month.

5. It's only money. How can you put a price tag on personal freedom and expression?

6. I'm having fun; don't spoil the moment by looking at the bill.

7. I'll be so rich by the time the payment is due.

8. It's a long-term investment.

9. I'm not spoiled. I just need it now!

10. This will never go out of style.

I've since posted my list of self-deception on my Frugal Duchess blog, and I've taken that list with me all these years. My list prompted other writers to contribute their favorite list of self lies. Here's the list posted by Kimber, a blogger at No Limits Ladies (*www.NoLimitsLadies.com*).

Kimber's List of Spending Lies

1. The stock will go back up.

2. It's an investment piece of clothing.

3. I could always sell that piece of art/antique/collectible for more than I bought it for.

4. The opportunity might not come again.

5. Just this once.

6. I don't have time to shop around.

7. His advice has always been solid.

8. If I'm going to be an author, I should buy books.

9. She's my mom; she needs it.

10. Christmas only comes once a year.

With such spending habits, it's no surprise that many consumers have trouble saving for homes, emergencies or other long-time goals. Twenty-eight percent of survey participants reported that they have zero funds left over after paying basic living expenses, according to a recent ACNielsen survey. "The U.S. is number one when it comes to the percentage of the population that claims to have no spare cash," according to the survey.

Nobody's fault but mine

It's not my parents' fault that I became a spendthrift. They raised me with practical and traditional values about money and work. And my parents backed up their verbal messages with hard work. For instance, during the normal work week my father taught elementary school—but at night he worked jobs at a high-end restaurant, a supper club, a small boutique, and for a while at the docks in Philadelphia, where he unloaded cargo from ships in the late evening and pre-dawn hours.

What's more, I believed my parents when they preached: "Money doesn't grow on trees." But I also saw and heard the secret messages that danced through our lives. Sure, money came from hard work, but money also appeared like magic. And even as a little girl I tuned into an odd frequency of fantasy and wishful thinking.

I had seen evidence of this Magic Money in my parents' lives. For example, when I was seven years old, my father won the grand prize in a Knights of Columbus sweepstakes. After teaching all day and lifting heavy restaurant trays at night, my dad was tired and gave in easily when a fellow waiter pressed him to buy the last ticket in a raffle book.

After signing the stub, my dad quickly forgot about the sweepstakes until a telegram announced that my parents had won a three-month trip around the world—an extravagant package during the mid-1960s. My parents—who had taken my brother Ben and me to see the 1964 New York World's Fair—were quite tempted by the idea of a summer world tour. But reality set in before they packed their bags.

First, they were reluctant to give up the extra income earned by teaching summer school for the Philadelphia School District. Second, there was the high cost of live-in childcare for me and my siblings; and third, my parents realized that the three-month tour would involve additional traveling expenses that would take a big bite out of the new home that they were building in South Jersey. And with the closing date less than a year away, they were worried about the settlement costs related to their dream home. Ultimately, my parents opted to take the cash substitute for the grand prize. It was a prudent decision based on thrifty principals. But that's not what I told my classmates during a show-and-tell presentation.

"My M&D won thousands and thousands of dollars in a raffle, and that's how we're going to pay for our new house," I announced to the class.

Listening to that tale, the teacher smiled. I could tell that she thought I had made the whole thing up. But it didn't matter to me. I knew the truth: Money didn't grow on trees, but if you wished hard enough, money appeared like magic.

Time to grow up

It took me awhile to stop believing that some fairy, angel or magical g-dmother would sprinkle my bank account with pixie dust or leave a stack of gold bricks under my pillow while I spent the night dreaming.

I wish that I could tell you that I gave up such fantasies during my twenties. But here's the truth: I didn't find my brain until I was 30. In fact, if I could write off any decade in my life, I would probably write-off my 20s. At 18, I should have just taken a 12-year-age deficit, re-financed my youth and then fast-forwarded to 31. That's when I became smarter about money.

But if I had not been so stupid about money (and other things) at 20, I would not be wiser now. Here are five things from my 20s that I no longer do:

1. I no longer straighten my hair with expensive chemically-induced salon treatments that cost about $3,000 a year. (Plus interest because I usually used plastic for salon visits.)

The worst part: I even paid a fortune for straight hair when I had no groceries.

Even worse: I straightened my hair because I had a bad self-image. (Straightened hair is fine, if you just like the look. But that wasn't my story.) A better self image has saved me a ton of money.

2. I've nixed the weekly manicures. I have paid $500 to $1,500 annually for a service that would have cost about $3 a year based on the price of a bottle of nail enamel. I should have put that money in a 401(k) plan. It's like this: Nails break and the polish chips, but money appreciates!

3. Credit card meals. Hey, I'm 49 and I still have indigestion from all those Manhattan meals from the 1980s. Chewing plastic, with those magnetic strips caught in your gums—painful!

4. Buy-One-Get-Two (in every color!). This is not a joke. One day, in New York, I went to every Ann Taylor in Manhattan—from the Upper West Side to Wall Street. I hunted down a shirt on sale. Found the shirt; found the sale; found every color.

5. Shopping while hungry, angry, depressed, rejected or in Paris with no money.

I think a lot about past spending trips and expensive restaurant meals, as I sit on the balcony of my apartment located on one of the small islands that comprise Miami Beach. Financially, I'm on my own island of fiscal recovery, with a solid concrete wall sitting staunchly between me and my Dream House.

Like my father and mother, I've been working overtime to build a solid foundation for a family home. Occasionally I buy a lottery or raffle ticket, but I've found my magic ticket in frugal living in a very Southern City.

Frugal habits are a popular topic in the community of personal finance bloggers. Members of my online community, for example, contributed our personal lists of 25 Frugal Habits. Here's my list:

The Best of Me: 25 Frugal Things I Do

1. Dilute dishwashing soaps, shampoos and liquid hand soaps with water.

2. Rinse my hair with organic apple cider vinegar (great low-cost conditioner).

3. Split meals in restaurants with my children and husband.

4. Bring my own food to theme parks. (Some parks permit DIY snacks.)

5. Drink filtered water from my kitchen sink.

6. Rarely order drinks in restaurants.

7. Complete many errands by walking. It's a two-for-one exercise.

8. Use public transportation.

9. Rip paper towels in half.

10. Use inexpensive hair-grooming products that are also on sale.

11. Style and cut my own hair.

12. Often stay with friends and relatives while on vacation.

13. Combine coupons with weekly sale promotions and only buy items I would have purchased at full price.

14. Purchase organic vegetables through a food co-op.

15. Stock up on non-perishable sale items.

16. Buy generic or private label products.

17. Make cards for birthdays and holidays.

18. Recycle gift bags and wrapping paper.

19. Shop online for discount travel deals.

20. Streamline my makeup and skincare routine.

21. Take advantage of end-of-season garment sales.

22. Shop in used bookstores and thrift stores.

23. Purchase cosmetics in drugstores.

24. Crush my own beans and make my own gourmet coffee.

25. Try to avoid shops and malls as much as possible. FD

The Duchess and
the Great Depression

With phone, feet and keyboard, I've spent hours research-ing my Dream House. My fact-finding mission has yielded details about past sales, renovations and the age of the property. For instance, from public real estate tax records, I've discovered that the Mediterranean received a major facelift in 1984 and that's when—I believe—the Master Bedroom suite was probably added. The size and the luxury of that second floor suite—with its large balcony, indoor spa, and walk-in closet—have a 1980s vibe.

Subsequent owners have repainted, re-landscaped and rearranged the property. But the foundation was built in 1934. Like my Dream House, the foundation of my life was shaped by that same decade. The twin forces of the Depression Era—thriftiness—and the product-driven prosperity of the Baby Boom years were my childhood companions. In fact, I am the Frugal Duchess because my parents—born in 1932 (dad) and 1936 (mom)—were children during the largest economic downturn in U.S. history, and became parents during one of the greatest wealth-generating eras of our country.

On the one hand, my parents were very frugal. On the other hand, they also gave us so much: Disney World vacations, happy birthday parties and Broadway play dates in Manhattan. In short, I have always felt like royalty—call me Duchess—because I have had two childhoods: my own and the dream childhood that my parents never had, including school years laced with new shoes.

Straight-from-the box footwear was in short supply during my parents' childhood. On a farm in Virginia, for example, my father spent one summer without shoes when his elderly caregiver—a great aunt who was half blind—mistakenly purchased two left shoes for my dad. The store was far from their rural home, and so my father wore two left shoes. But most of the time—especially in the summer—he ran around in bare feet.

On the streets of Philadelphia, my mother had shoes, but they were old and repeatedly repaired by her father, Frank Stephens, a Philadelphia-based tailor and shoe cobbler. My grandfather, a short bald man, was talented with needles, cloth, and leather and had a famous clientele of black entertainers, such as Pearl Bailey, local politicians and some Philly mobsters, according to family tales.

His clients appreciated my grandpop's repair skills, but my mother simply wished for shoes that weren't fixed over and over again with hot glue and leather. From this my mother did learn the value of carefully preserving and maintaining possessions, and to this day my parents' garage is filled with well-preserved books, photos and family papers. My mom and her brother—my Uncle Frankie—also inherited a bit of Grandpop's skills and crafts, spending a lot of time making up games and earning extra pocket money.

"I was always enterprising," my mother once told me. "One year I sold carnations on the street for Mother's Day."

Meme's Story:
Saving String and Money

When I talk about the frugal tips that I've picked up from my parents and grandparents, I'm always reminded of my friend Leah, a twenty-something mother, who lives by the frugal advice she got from her grandmother. Felisa Tzvia Linder, also known as Meme, was born in Argentina in the early 1900s. Meme died a few years ago, but Leah shared her story with me.

"She taught me that nothing needs to be wasted and everything can be used," Leah said. "It doesn't mean that you're serving leftovers every night. If you do it properly you can make beautiful dishes from odds and ends."

Her grandmother, for instance, used small leftover servings of fresh vegetable salad to enhance a quiche or to spice up a soup. Likewise, after opening canned fruit or vegetables, Linder would freeze and save the clear juice from those cans. The liquid contents from the vegetables doubled as a base for homemade soups, and sweet juice and syrups were used to spice up cakes or compote recipes.

With such sparks of creativity and frugality, Meme found uses for leftover bread (bread pudding) and even the remains of loose tea, which were mixed with plant soil in the garden.

And she never signed birthday or greeting cards. Instead she placed her signature and private messages on pieces of paper that were slipped into blank cards. In that fashion, a single card could be used repeatedly and the personalized birthday message could be stocked away for safe-keeping. She saved string and threads (for small sewing jobs) and other odds and ends. Despite her thrifty ways, Meme believed in quality.

"When she bought something she would always buy the best so that it would last," her granddaughter said.

Above all, Meme was generous with her money. Whatever she saved on juice and string, she offered to her children, grandchildren and great grandchildren.

"She taught me so much. When I'm making a recipe that she taught me, I feel her working the dough," Leah said. "It's a real blessing."

Dollar Stores and the Depression

In addition to all the sage advice I've received from my parents and grandparents, one of my favorite shopping concepts is the dollar store, which has roots in the Depression era. Dollar General, for example, was founded in 1939.

Dollar General founders J. L. Turner and Cal Turner of Kentucky opened a whoesale operation, that was converted into a dollar retail store in the 1950s. From the 1950s through the 1980s, the dollar store concept exploded, according to the company's website.

From low-tech kitchen gadgets to shiny lip gloss, a good dollar store can yield an armful of treasured savings. Whether the Dollar General of old, or the dollar stores of today, the point of these stores is in helping consumers save money.

Consider my latest shopping coup. For 100 pennies, plus tax, my husband purchased a cell phone charger for the car that works quite well. The price was well-below the $19.95 price tag sported by a comparable model at a local electronics store. Our recent spree also yielded a cute but funky napkin holder, a trendy pair of tropical flip-flops, shiny aloe-based lip gloss, bedroom slippers, and a few gooey, rubber yo-yos that execute several unusual tricks while blinking like disco lights.

These items have passed the ultimate test. For example, a pair of fashion-savvy teenage girls inquired about my lip gloss. And on a recent train trip, a 9-year-old boy and his 7-year-old sister kept pestering my sons for the dollar store yo-yos they were holding. Now that's a sure sign of success.

I'm not the only dollar store fan out there. My friend Ellen purchases a wide assortment of merchandise and hair products from different dollar stores in South Florida. At those stores, Ellen has purchased everything from kitchen strainers to a decorative paper Japanese lantern for her home. And whereas a typical shopping trip with children can be an emotional and financial drain, the stakes are considerably lower in a dollar store, Ellen said. Dollar stores can provide a fun outing for children.

"It makes them feel like the world is their oyster," she said. "It's one of the few stores where you can walk in and know you can afford something."

Of course, not all dollar stores are created equal. Some locations are filled with overruns of quality merchandise and others, quite frankly, are filled with junk. What's more, some of the so-called bargains at dollar stores may be more expensive than weekly specials at retail chains. To get the best value, my husband and I follow these informal rules:

Think small. If you are uncertain about an item, buy one as a sample. If satisfied, go back and stock up.

Stay informed. Know your prices and keep track of value. Not every item in a dollar store is worth a dollar. Sometimes the unit price is actually the same or higher than other stores.

Shop around. Some dollar stores specialize in different items. One store may carry excellent paper goods, whereas another may specialize in kitchen items.

Don't be a snob. Would that merchandise appeal to you at an expensive boutique? Don't let low price be a barrier.

We've even purchased pet supplies for Scruffy—our dog—at a dollar store in South Beach. Of course, we could have spent a fortune on pet supplies and trinkets at an expensive boutique near our home, where dog shampoos and conditioners cost about $20 a bottle and doggy outfits cost over $100.

One Buck Bargains For the Dog

1. Great nylon leashes

2. Really cute dog bowls (one for water, one for food)

3. A package of chew sticks (Other stores charge $6 to $7 for similar packages)

4. Assorted chew toys (I've seen the same toys for about $10 each)

5. Conditioning pet shampoo $1 for 16 fluid ounces versus high-end pet grooming products for $20 a bottle

Doggie Dollar Duds

1. Chain link leash. Scruffy hates this one. So we don't use it.

2. Rope/Ball-tug-of-war toy. It was not well-made and my dog quickly ripped it apart.

3. Spiky rubberized teething circle. He ignores this toy.

Food from the Dollar Store

We buy some of our groceries from the dollar store, and we're not alone. Many dollar stores have an interesting assortment of food items, and I know of at least one dollar store that sells fresh produce. From our local dollar stores, we have purchased Kedem Grape Juice for 50 cents (full price about $6), chips, cookies and canned goods.

Here's how we shop for food in dollar stores:

Check dates. I look for expiration dates, sell-by dates and best-if-used-by dates.

Study the packaging. If the item looks "gently worn," we put it back on the shelf.

Price check. Know the actual price at a grocery store and recent sale prices.

Buy-one/try-one. After wasting money on a batch of stale snacks, we taste-test dollar store deals first. We buy a sample. If it's either stale or hated by the family, we obviously don't purchase more.

Stock up. When my husband found our brand of grape juice for 50 cents (down from $6), he really stocked up and bought $40 worth, which lasted us for a year.

One of my readers wrote, "If you really like an item, make sure you purchase it ASAP or even stock up, because the [dollar store] may never have it again. My favorite bargain is picture frames at Dollar Tree. Anytime they have a new shipment, I stock up for gifts, for the office, and home. From experience, they usually never have the same frame twice."

I've learned to be cautious about buying water from dollar stores. At one dollar store, the water bottles were super cheap, but I could taste the plastic in the water. Maybe the bottles were on the shelf too long. We try to avoid bottled water anyway and now have a filter on our kitchen faucet, but when I do purchase bottled water it's not from a dollar store.

Bulk shopping

Many adults who grew up during the Depression like to purchase home and cooking supplies in large quantities. But bulk shopping is also a popular sport for many celebrities of all ages.

For example, one national magazine featured a snapshot of Adam Sandler pushing a large cart filled with "family-sized packages of Charmin, Brawny paper towels, Coke, Diet Coke and Diet Dr. Pepper." But based on my own shopping experiences and Adam Sandler's shopping cart, I've developed these rules for bulk shopping.

Skip the national brands. Sandler's purchases consisted of many name brand items. Unless there's a super cheap sale, I usually skip the name brands. Many so-called private label, store-brand or generic products are produced in the same factories as the big-ticket name-brand versions. The only difference: you're not paying more for celebrity endorsements and national campaigns.

Buy large quantities. I like Sandler's jumbo shopping binge. Save time, gas, and money, by scooping up lots of products at one time.

Watch per-unit costs. Not every jumbo package represents the best deal. Sometimes a smaller package offers the biggest money-saving option. Do the math before stocking up on the jumbo bundles.

And if you're having trouble calculating unit prices, turn on your cell phone, advises Mapgirl, one of my fellow personal finance bloggers:

"The killer app on a cell phone is the CALCULATOR. I can't promote that enough. Never complain you can't do the math on unit pricing. It's often right on the shelf if you read the tag. If you can't, whip out the phone and figure it out," Mapgirl told me.

From maid's room to pantry

My bulk shopping trips would multiply in volume if I owned the Mediterranean because I would turn the Maid's Room into a storage area, filled with nonperishables at discount prices. That's a trick I learned from a frugal friend, who has turned odd corners of her home—window seats, linen closets and other random spaces—into revenue-saving storage pockets.

My kids, of course, have other ideas. Equipped with DVDs, CDs, iPods and Xbox controllers, they'd love to turn the small suite near the kitchen into a 'tween/teen recreation area—complete with its own entrance to the streets. I don't think so. I plan to claim the space for a home office or convert the Maid's Room into a storage room for my bulk shopping purchases. Those are a few of my fantasies.

Outlet shopping adventures

In addition to bulk shopping at warehouse malls or big box super-stores, outlet shopping is another popular frugal strategy in many parts of the country. When I moved to Miami Beach as a wife and new mom, I was lost in the shopping aisles of trendy boutiques and I didn't know my shopping options.

Another young mom in my neighborhood—a serious shopper and also a transplant from New York—kindly offered to take me to her favorite shopping district: Sawgrass Mills Outlet Mall, a super outlet mall located about 40 minutes from Miami (depending on traffic). So, my husband and I (with a toddler in tow!) naively accompanied Ms. Marathon Shopper to Sawgrass Mall. We found great bargains, like a pair of brown denim designer jeans for our 18-month old son and a white dress shirt for my husband—both at a great price. And there were dishes, shoes, comforters, coats, dresses and framed art for the home.

Dazed, hungry and confused, we followed Ms. Marathon Shopper for hours into nearly all of the 400 stores and entertainment shops at Sawgrass Mall. I made a decision that day: No more outlet shopping for me!

Armed with a plan

More than 15 years later, I still have not returned to Sawgrass Mall, and I have avoided just about every outlet mall I've come across. But my experience—and potential savings—would have been different if I had shopped with a plan.

The plan idea is sage advice that comes from Kenneth Thomas, a national banking analyst. Thomas—who shops at outlet stores around the country—is a man with a personal and professional mission. As a bank consultant, he analyzes potential bank branch locations around the country and has visited traditional malls, strip shopping centers, and outlet stores throughout the U.S. What's more, his professional shopping duties have merged into a personal ethic when outlet shopping.

"You just don't walk around aimlessly," said Thomas. "You stay focused. You do your business and you leave."

On a regular basis, Thomas—a fairly wealthy man with expensive tastes—shops at outlet malls in Florida, New York, New Jersey, Virginia and other states. He purchases shoes, suits, sweaters and other items with a minimal investment of time or money. (He once purchased a pair of $500 Italian shoes for $100.) On a typical shopping trip, Thomas avoids peak hours and completes his duties within 15 minutes. He loves buying costly items for a fraction of the normal retail price. Thomas shared his strategies with me.

Outlet Strategies

Shop with a list. Know exactly what you need and don't get scattered by veering from your target. Aimless shopping wastes time and money.

Limit your store selection. Thomas vetoes marathon shopping trips. On a typical shopping venture, he sticks to a short list of two or three stores.

Park carefully. Many large outlet stores have their own exits to the parking lot. A direct path to individual stores provides convenience and limits temptations. "It's all in the parking," Thomas said.

Avoid interior corridors and hallways. Use the parking lot and exterior doors to hop from store to store. With that strategy, you'll avoid unnecessary purchases of ice cream cones, nose-clipping scissors and other spur-of-the moment trinkets. You'll also avoid the mind-numbing crowds.

Go straight to the clearance section. Many outlet stores—such as Off 5TH, Saks Fifth Avenue's outlet—are stocked with clearance items from the parent chain. But even within those discount stores, there are special clearance sections with additional savings of 20 to 70 percent off the ticket price, Thomas said.

"The clearance area within [a clearance outlet store] is like a double discount," Thomas said. "You just have to stay focused to manage your time and money."

Know your prices. By window-shopping online, you can research the best deals before leaving your home. There are many excellent online shopping portals that provide a range of prices and the best deals for a given item.

Yard Sales

If given a choice between a yard sale and an outlet mall, I would choose the mom-and-pop version of a flea market. I love yard sales. From an antique pearl collar for $1 to a $1,200 Italian wool suit for $15, my husband and I have found great bargains at yard sales.

Even celebrities have hit the flea market/garage sale/yard sale circuit. At one time on You Tube (*www.youtube.com*)—for example—you could find Oprah, the billionaire television queen, buying two dolls for two dollars at a Midwest garage sale.

Likewise, the global electronic village includes news of Kirstie Alley, actress and former Jenny Craig pitchwoman, peddling a huge sculpture of French fries, silver tone bar stools and a spotted dog statue at her own yard sale.

Even Imelda Marcos—shoe diva and former First Lady of the Philippines—now prowls flea markets for odd trinkets that she fashions into jewelry for her new low-priced "The Imelda Collection."

I've found the best stuff in the waterfront mansions of Miami Beach, where pop stars like Jennifer Lopez, members of the Bee Gees and Ricky Martin have lived. At one yard sale, for example, my husband and I picked up a large stack of Ralph Lauren cloth dinner napkins—all new—in various colors and patterns for 50 cents each. The seller had originally purchased the napkins for a dinner party. However, before the event, she repeatedly changed her mind about the color scheme.

Stuck with dozens of unused napkins, the party planner sold the merchandise at her "garage sale." As a bonus, she threw in elegant napkins rings in different sizes and shapes for 25 cents each. We were the lucky buyers. Using cloth napkins has saved us a bundle on paper goods and created a festive look for our own dinner parties.

But my passion for yard sales involves more than just great stuff at great prices. Garage sales and estate auctions also offer informal tours and an insider's glimpse of many neighborhoods throughout the country. In fact, when my husband and I relocated from Manhattan to Miami during the mid-1990s, we made friends and learned the local landscape by traveling around to different yard sales in South Beach and the Greater Miami area.

My Top 5 Favorite Garage Sale Finds

Little Space Aliens. A bucket of little rubber action figures for about $2 on Pine Tree Drive—near a golf course—in Miami Beach. This great find came in especially handy when my house was hit by the chicken pox. While sick, my oldest son (about 4 years old at the time) played with the space aliens for hours. And the little rubber toys held up well in the bath tub.

Zeniga suit. A beautiful Italian wool suit (typically sells for $1,200) for my husband for $15. On a little island across from the Port of Miami, Avi and I pulled into a garage sale that was winding down. During a friendly chat, the garage sale proprietor sized up Avi and then ran into his home and pulled out the Zeniga suit, which happens to be my husband's favorite suit label.

Little Tikes car. List price: about $60. Gently used model at garage sale: $5. The Little Tikes car—hard plastic vehicle in primary colors— is the hottest selling car in the world (Really!). We had wanted one for our children for some time and were elated to find this toy car at a garage sale on Alton Road. Garage sales are great places for picking up children's toys—especially durable plastic items from Fisher-Price and Little Tikes.

First Edition Lord of the Rings Trilogy. Long before the Hobbits hit the big screen, Avi and I stumbled across a first edition, boxed set of the Lord of the Rings Trilogy by Tolkien for $10 at a yard sale. Avi was a big fan of the series and I quickly became enamored with the Middle Earth tale. Our version includes a super pull-out map and the author's annotated notes about the text.

My Blue Suit. Two-piece, light wool suit, with an A-line skirt $20. The suit belonged to an older woman, who—I believe—had Alzheimer's or some illness that demanded 24/7 care. The contents of her Miami Beach home were sold through her daughter. As a tiny woman, I have trouble finding clothes that fit. So I was amazed when the suit fit as if it were custom-made for me. FD

The Maid's Room and Getting What You Pay For

At least once a month, bright yellow balloons and bold signs announce the arrival of an open house party for prospective buyers at my Dream House. I am a regular guest at those parties and the real estate brokers know me by name. After all this time I know the property as if it were my own. For instance, I know where to find the hidden entrance to the Maid's Room. It's a door that looks like any other closet, but leads to a tiny suite adjacent to the kitchen.

The Maid's Room, the smallest bedroom in the house, moves me. That's because both of my grandmothers were maids. When they began working during the 1930s, domestic work was one of the few occupations widely open to Black women. Even the grandmother of billionaire

Oprah Winfrey worked as a maid, the superstar told the audience in her 2007 commencement address at Howard University.

Likewise, during the 1950s, my mother worked as a weekend nanny while attending college. And even I—the pampered suburban princess— spent the summer of 1979 pushing a mop and rag as part of the house- keeping staff at Georgetown University, where I attended school. It was a short-term gig, with free room and board—a Maid's Room, of course— in the university dorm.

So in an odd sort of way, the Maid's Room in my Dream House feels like home to me. I fantasize about turning that room into my own South Beach-style writer's studio, where I will write stories about my grand- mothers. I could—for example—write for days about the bargain-hunt- ing exploits of my maternal grandmother. Sometimes, I even imagine her in my shopping cart as I hunt down unit prices. Clearly, those Southern women rent a lot of space in my head.

Not your ordinary grandmothers

Nobody I know—black, white, brown or other—can claim grandmothers like mine. My grandmothers—beautiful and mysterious—were always running somewhere. Between the two of them, they moved from six homes, four states, two legal husbands, one common-law husband, one tomato farm, one tailor shop and nine children, including my parents— the youngest of each family.

My dad was three months old in 1932 when his mother, Gertrude Beatrice ("Bea") King Harvey left my grandfather's tomato farm in Vir- ginia. Country life (no indoor plumbing, paved roads or other conven- iences of my grandmother's affluent childhood home in Baltimore) must have been a shock for Bea. And she shocked everyone by running away.

When she ran away after 10 years of marriage, my grandmother was only 28 and had already given birth to eight children, including my dad—who was an infant at that time. Everyone has a theory, (economic pressure, her well-to-do family's disapproval of her marriage, post-par- tum depression or personal turmoil), but no one knows for sure why my grandmother left her husband—a handsome Black veteran from World War I and a tomato farmer.

Meanwhile, in 1938, my mother was two when Julia Wardlaw

Stephens—her mother and a pulpit preacher—left my grandfather. He was a tailor, who allegedly ran his own speakeasy bar for celebrities and party-goers during Prohibition and later. No one knows why my maternal grandparents—the church lady and the speakeasy tailor—married, and no one knows why they separated.

Julia was not a typical grandmother. She didn't bake, wear glasses or smell like talcum powder. But she did make coffee that smelled better than chocolate chip cookies. She wore high heels and fox stoles. Julia was movie-star-beautiful, like Dorothy Dandridge. With her high cheekbones, sharp nose and pressed hair, Julia could have been one of those models in old issues of *Ebony* magazine.

And most importantly, Julia was a preacher—a lady pastor with her own church, Mount Tabor, in North Philly. She was—according to family legend—the first Black woman in Philadelphia to have her own church. No one could deliver the Word like Julia and even when she stuttered, she'd pull you along as if she were holding your hand in a crowded subway. And you'd never want to let go, when Julia Stephens was in the pulpit.

Not always a bargain

Julia also enjoyed shopping, and she especially loved buying anything on sale: Halloween candy in November, chocolate Santas in January and two-for-one boxes of Valentine candy for Easter. Her purchases were sometimes stale, but always sweet. My brother, sisters and I loved Grandmom's gifts.

Some of her bargain finds were wonderful—she loved buying coffee on sale—and others were disastrous. For instance, I remember a time when my grandmother purchased boxes and boxes of Halloween candy that were on sale long after the holiday.

Unfortunately, that candy sale offered more tricks than treats. That's because the chocolate nugget filling also contained worms and we became sick. (Over 40 years later, I still remember the sight of the infested candy.) Irate, my mother and my grandmother filed a lawsuit against the grocery store, which was part of a large regional chain in the Philadelphia area. Ultimately, the judge called it a nuisance suit, but awarded my mother and grandmother a settlement of a few hundred dollars.

Of course, to my childhood eyes, it seemed like the money—an unexpected financial bonus—appeared like magic. It was like *Charlie and the Chocolate Factory*, but our "Golden Ticket" was shaped like small worms. However, I did learn two practical lessons from the Halloween candy episode:

Buyer beware. Carefully screen post-holiday sales for defects. Check the expiration dates on all food products. Inspect everything you eat.

File complaints. Of course, a lawsuit is not the answer to every faulty purchase. But there's no reason to accept shoddy merchandise or service.

Speak up

It pays to complain if your concerns are valid and honest. There is an art to whining. You can get a lot of mileage out of consumer complaints filed with a combination of good cheer and forcefulness. There is no reason to accept poor service or problem merchandise, including toys that arrive at a store "dead-on-arrival."

Likewise, substandard vacation accommodations (dirty rooms or unfulfilled promises) can also be appealed to resort owners or your credit card company if you are dissatisfied.

An honest complaint (without fabrications, embellishments or other unethical breaches) can yield coupons, vouchers or refunds if you have mastered the art of polite complaints. In my household, we go straight to the source when we have a consumer complaint. When dealing with products from a large manufacturer, we locate the 800 number and file our complaint with the appropriate consumers' relations department. From defective wheels on baby carriages to mislabeled cosmetics, we have found that most manufacturers are quite receptive to our feedback and have shipped—free of charge—parts, coupons and refunds for defective items.

In some cases, the manufacturer is more receptive to our complaints than even the retailers who directly sold us the goods. That's because many manufacturers seek to build brand loyalty and consumer confidence. They want your repeat business.

The important thing is to not abuse the process or the customer service operators, said one consumer rep for a major toy company, who gave me the inside-story on the complaint business. She estimates that 50 percent of callers are impolite or abusive and that attitude can carry hidden penalties for the consumer. For while her company is generous with its return and refund policy, callers that abuse the system are placed in a "restricted area."

Of course, every caller is theoretically treated the same, but exceptions can be made for those who abuse the system. The company—one of the largest manufacturers of children's toys—typically provides vouchers for consumers who have purchased defective toys or those missing parts. For amounts of $25 or under you do not even have to return the toy, but for refunds of larger amounts, the manufacturer will request a proof of purchase, including the return of some small, obscure part. For example, the company may request that you ship them the battery cover or some other part of the toy, the consumer rep said.

However, because abusive or repeat callers seeking freebies have been placed on a special restricted list they may receive fewer benefits. Keep in mind that if you give personal data in order to receive a voucher or a replacement part that information is logged into the system.

"We monitor every call," she said. "Everything is documented and monitored."

Ask for store discounts!

When you shop in a store, don't be shy about asking for lower prices when purchasing everyday items and gadgets. Consider this: when shopping for cars, most consumers have a back-and-forth talk with the dealer over the price. Now apply that same logic to shopping sprees in major chains and smaller stores.

For example, when purchasing a portable DVD player for one of our sons, we asked the store manager about future promotions for DVD players. We figured we would just wait for the lower price. "Hey, if the only thing holding you back is the price, I can go lower," the store manager said. He offered the player for $119 and my husband accepted!

The manager also explained to us that peers at his store and many others have the authority to cut deals with inquiring consumers!

Price-matching strategies

Knowledge about store price-matching programs and other customer services can translate into significant savings. Price matching is a process in which one store matches or beats the advertised prices of its competitors.

This price-matching service is typically offered by major discount chains, pharmacy outlets and appliance stores. Even some local dry cleaners will let you cash in on savings from competing coupon offers. National office supply stores are also willing to beat their competitors' prices for goods ranging from paper products to big-ticket home-office furniture.

However, to take advantage of this wide universe of savings you need to stay current on the various prices offered by different retailers, said Beth, who is an ardent comparison shopper. For various products—ranging from tablecloths to toys—Beth tracks prices and timing of sales and promotions.

Celebrities are consumers, too

When Jessica Simpson was busy promoting the movie, *The Dukes of Hazzard*, she tracked down a price adjustment at Barneys, according to *In Touch* magazine. The magazine reported that Simpson requested a price adjustment when a pair of shoes she purchased at Barneys was subsequently discounted by 40 percent. Her savings—according to *In Touch*—was $200.

A representative for Jessica Simpson could not confirm the story and referred me to Barneys. I spoke to Kimberly Oser, a New York-based spokesman for the store. Citing, customer confidentiality Oser declined to comment on the discounted shoes. However, in a subsequent email, she provided details about Barneys price adjustment policy.

"Price adjustments are given within seven days of the original purchase date. The merchandise must be present in order to process the adjustment," Oser wrote.

Other major retailers, ranging from Home Depot to Old Navy have similar policies. Meanwhile, many stores also have generous return and exchange policies. Based on my research, Bloomingdales and Macy's have generous return policies. Receipts are not required, according to Lisa Kauffman, senior vice president for marketing in the Florida Division of Macy's.

"We believe that a properly handled return is a good investment. It supports future business," Kauffman said.

Trapped in a Walk-in Closet

My Dream House has a private staircase that leads to a huge suite of rooms on the second floor. This suite—the master bedroom—consists of a spacious private balcony, a bathroom that rivals any South Beach Day Spa, and a walk-in closet twice the size of my kitchen. That huge space gives my 12-year-old son ideas.

"Mommy," he said. "When we buy the house, this could be your office."

He's right. The walk-in closet is private, cozy and convenient. When I'm stressed out, I can jump into the Jacuzzi in the spa area; when I need fresh air, I can lounge on the nearby balcony. And there's ample room for a desk, filing cabinets, and my multiplying piles of papers. But there are no windows. It is, after all, just a closet. And with a silent nod to novelist E.M. Forster, I try to explain that I need a *Room with a View.*

"I can't work in a room without windows," I tell my son. "I want the Maid's Room."

The massive master-bedroom closet, however, haunts me. And I feel guilty because I know that the secluded walk-in closet would be an ideal work-space for an easily distracted writer like me. And the Maid's Room—with its easy access to kitchen snacks—would be a perfect play-room/entertainment center for the children.

But beyond the family politics of space, I also feel guilty because I want that closet for storage. In fact, I am convinced that I need that space. And honestly, I have enough clothes, shoes, purses, and junk to fill a closet that is almost larger than our first apartment in New York City. Trapped in the master bedroom of my Dream House, I face the truth about my bargain-hunting: I own too much stuff.

And I'm not alone. Nearly 70 percent of consumers pray for more closet space, according to a survey of over 4,000 readers published in *O, The Oprah Magazine.*

Here's a summary of the results:

>60 percent of poll participants have NOT viewed the rear of their closet in months.

>10 percent confessed to buying a new garment at least once a week.

>31 percent own 10 pairs of jeans.

>12 percent own over 50 pairs of shoes.

Every year, consumers in the U.S. spend billions of dollars on new clothing. And the pressure to spend is felt by all of us, including celebrities. For instance, Carrie Underwood, the 2005 American Idol winner, faced over-the-top spending suggestions when she was a contestant on the talent show.

"I had my battles with the *American Idol* stylist because he always wanted me to buy real expensive things," Carrie told one magazine. "I was like, 'My mama raised me right. I can't spend $400 on a pair of jeans!'"

Retail therapy

Unlike Carrie Underwood, I have succumbed to the elusive lure of retail therapy. What is retail therapy anyway? Call it New-Stuff Happiness or the short-term buzz of a good feeling sparked by shopping. Under pressure—home, work and money—I have taken heavy doses of retail therapy. During one therapy session, for instance, I fell for a pitch from a national clothing chain: With every purchase of $50 in merchandise, shoppers would receive $25 in free clothing. So after buying about $100 in marked-downs, I was ready for $50 in free clothing and accessories. Not so fast. The $50 discount applied to a future shopping trip, the cashier explained, smiling patiently as if she had repeated the same mantra all day long.

I smiled back—patiently—and looked forward to my next shopping trip, with the promise of free merchandice. Not so fast. To collect on $50 in freebies, I would have to spend another qualifying $100. At that point, I really saved a lot. I left the store, while my so-called free merchandise stayed on the shelf. Clearly, a bargain is not always a good deal.

Meanwhile, the shopping aisles are filled with fellow shoppers, who, like me, have failed to read the fine print. One of my newspaper editors, for example, once shopped at a major retail store, with coupons for hefty discounts on big-ticket items. But her potential savings turned to dust, when she discovered that many brand names and products, including items on her list, were excluded from the advertised savings.

Based on that example and many other hit-and-miss shopping exploits, I've put together this warning list of shopping pitfalls.

Buy-one-get-one-half-off. Don't fall for this promotion, unless you really need an extra pair of shoes, another sweater or an additional pair of frosted sunglasses. Otherwise, it makes more sense to buy just one item.

Rebate offers. To save money from this type of promotion, you really need organization. That's because collecting rebate savings often depends on tracking deadlines, collecting random documents (receipts, bar codes and billing statements), and standing on your head while balancing a shopping cart. If you can do all that: Fine! But if, like me, you have trouble tracking a cumbersome paper trail or finding stamps by a postmark deadline, it's best to look for specials where the savings are immediately delivered at the cash register.

Alterations and accessories required. A deal is not a deal if a new garment requires either expensive alterations or a new wardrobe. With that principle in mind, I've recently saved a lot of money by limiting my wardrobe to a small range of colors. A new garment has to match or complement my other stuff. And if it doesn't fit, I drop it.

Anti-binge strategies

There are other anti-binge strategies that have helped me, including the Shopping Pop Quiz that appeared in *Woman's Day* magazine from columnist Mary Hunt, author of *Debt-Proof Living*.

Before making a purchase, ask yourself:

1. Is this item really necessary? (If no, put it back on the shelf.)

2. Is it affordable? (If no, put it back.)

3. Do I own another item that will serve the same purpose? (If yes, don't buy.)

4. Is it possible to wait and buy a cheaper substitute later? (If yes, don't buy.)

5. Have I really shopped around for the best deal? (If no, don't buy.)

6. What happens if I delay this purchase? This is the trick question. (If you're not going to lose the home of your dreams, the perfect shoe or a night's sleep, forget it!)

Are you a compulsive shopper?

Likewise, *Bankrate.com* featured a "Compulsive Shopper Test," written by Olivia Mellan, a psychotherapist, money coach and author of *Over-*

coming Overspending: A Winning Plan for Spenders and Their Partners.
I spoke with Mellan, and here is her test:

Are you a compulsive shopper? Answer "often," "sometimes," "rarely"
or "never."

1. Do you buy things you want, whether or not you can
   afford them at the moment?

2. Do you have trouble saving money? If you have a little
   extra available to save or invest, do you tend to think
   of something you'd rather spend it on?

3. Do you buy things to cheer yourself up or to reward
   yourself?

4. Does more than a third of your income, not including
   rent or mortgage payments, go to pay bills?

5. Do you juggle bill paying because you always seem to
   be living on the edge financially?

6. Do you tend to keep buying more of your favorite
   things even if you don't have a specific need for them?

7. If you have to deny yourself or put off buying something you really want, do you feel intensely deprived,
   angry or upset?

If you answered "often" or "sometimes" to four or more questions,
you're probably a compulsive spender, especially if you answered
"often" or "sometimes" to the last question.

Stripping down to basics

The frugal movement is often accompanied by a push for simplicity—
featuring a streamlined, decluttered lifestyle. It's a back-to-basics push.

For example, Simplicity In Kansas, a fellow blogger (*www.simplic
ityinkansas.com*), has stripped his closet down to the bare essentials.
Here's how he conquered his closet monster.

♦ Shifted to natural fibers and away from dry clean-only

garments. This move decreased costs and helped the environment.

♦ Established a shoe limit of five pairs of shoes: two basic pairs for work, one for exercise, one for casual, one for fun. A shoe tree is a must.

♦ Cleaned out his closet by donating 70 percent of all items that he was not wearing to charity.

"So, my closet is much smaller, cleaner and without the 'run rate costs' of dry cleaning," Mr. Kansas told me in a written comment on my blog. "Also, I am getting more use out of the clothes I am wearing and feel better about my decisions."

Thrift store leaks

For many shoppers thrift stores are the answer to the problem of high-price shopping. But even thrift stores can become a dangerous addiction if you shop too much, according to a few friends who have pulled back from their jaunts to secondhand stores. They love thrift stores, garage sales and other secondhand markets. But a steady stream of small purchases can overstuff your closets, while leaving the bank account bare. Based on conversations and my own experiences, I've put together a warning list for thrift store shoppers.

You know that you've hit one too many thrift stores when ...

1. You recognize all of the antique dealers and professional buyers who pick through used items in order to resell the merchandise for 1000 percent markups at their own high-end stores.

2. Your garage looks like a storehouse for vintage lamp shades.

3. The used bookstore dealer calls you to request a specific title.

4. You have bins and bins of children's clothes sorted by size, color and gender.

5. You have so many bins of used books, clothes and trinkets that you have trouble finding what you need.

I've been purging the walk-in closet in my apartment with two goals:

1. I want to find the back of the closet and

2. I want to create room for a home office in my existing closet, which, I'm embarrassed to say, is almost half the size of my first Manhattan apartment.

I don't really need windows, and I don't really need my spacious Dream House, either. At least that's what I'm telling myself.

Smart shopping strategies

As grandparents, my parents have presented my children with many gifts, including great bargains from end-of-season sales. At one clearance sale at JCPenney, my mother purchased several party dresses for my daughter for under $10 each.

"These were first quality dresses for 40 to 75 percent off," my mother said. "It was a tip that I got from the beauty parlor. The ladies in the stylist salon brought in dresses and were showing them. And I said, 'Oh, I'm going to get some for my granddaughter.'"

My Mom's Shopping Bag		
Outfit	**Original Price**	**Clearance**
Bonnie Jean Dress	$ 44.99	$ 9.77
Disorderly Kid Dress	$ 39.99	$ 9.77
Beige Uniform Pants	$ 14.99	$ 1.00

Once a year, I buy 90 percent of my new wardrobe for the entire year, and I rarely pay retail at those end-of-season sales. Consider my favorite jacket from Ann Taylor Loft. The original price: $99 reduced to $39.99, then reduced to $29.99. I finally purchased the jacket for $15 at the 50 percent-off final clearance sale. Here's my strategy:

Find end-of-season sales. Summer clothes in September and winter clothes in January often sell for 75 to 90 percent off the full retail price.

Look for basic pieces. I've found new shirts for $1 to $5 at Marshalls and a blue tweed skirt for $6 at Ann Taylor.

Shop for quality. Personal finance blogger Flexo of Consumerism Commentary (*www.consumerismcommentary.com*) said that it's penny-wise, but pound-foolish to "buy the least expensive clothing and shoes." Why? The answer is simple. "Your clothing budget will suffer if you have to replace the wardrobe frequently because of poor quality," Flexo said.

Take fashion risks with accessories. At end-of-season sales, I've purchased new hats, bathing suits, sandals and other accessories at various stores for under $6.

Know your cost-per-wear

I get extra mileage out of my clothes by calculating costs-per-wear, a frugal strategy advocated in the business book *How to Say It For Women*, by Phyllis Mindell. Here's her example:

One businesswoman buys a Liberty of London shawl in 1986 at Harrods for $100. She wears the shawl about 10 times annually for 10 years, which translates into a "price per wear" value of under $1. Likewise, I have a black jersey skirt (originally $60 and reduced to $14.88) that costs only 50 cents per wear.

My Cost-Per-Wear Matrix			
Garment	Clearance Price	Number of Wears	Cost Per Wear
Black Jersey Skirt	$ 14.88	30	$ 0.50
Black T-Shirt	$ 6.88	50	$ 0.14
Silk Wrap Skirt	$ 29.00	20	$ 1.45

Over the next 12 months those cost-per-wear figures will drop, with the black skirt, for instance, dipping to 25 cents per wear. The skirt does not need dry cleaning, an expensive process that dramatically inflates the total cost of a garment and the price-per-wear estimate.

Of course, I've had my share of missteps. A few years ago, I purchased trendy shirts at a small discount chain for teens. Big mistake. The shirts were low-quality garments and due to the inferior fabric, the shirts did not wash well. Additionally, the trendy cut quickly went out of style. It was not my finest shopping moment.

The good news: I only spent $12 for each shirt. The bad news: I only wore each shirt a few times and my cost per wear was about $4. Fortunately, I'm getting a lot of low-cost mileage from the rest of my closet.

'You should be able to have affordable, quality fashion,' actress Sarah Jessica Parker told *People.com* as she recently launched her clothing line Bitten (every item for $19.98 and less) at Steve & Barry's chain store.

Low price for high-quality is one of the latest trends in high fashion, according to an industry forecast in the *Wall Street Journal* from Fashion Guru Tom Ford (formerly of Gucci).

"With Target, for example, you go in there and find something that is a great price and wonderful for its intrinsic value. This is democratization of fashion. I love this high-low concept," Ford said. "There is all this accessibility—everything is now online."

Signs of Cheap Chic as Spotted by The Wall Street Journal

- $69 frocks from designer Vera Wang, who usually makes red-carpet gowns (at eye-popping prices) for celebrities.

- Expansion of upscale designer names at low-priced stores such as Target and Wal-Mart.

- The popularity of high-fashion at low-ticket vendors such as H&M.

Here's more evidence: My newsroom editor bought a pair of elegant leather dress shoes for her job-seeking son for just under $30 at Target. The store is stocked with famous names such as Mossimo, Joy Gryson, Liz Lange, and architect Michael Graves and others. JCPenney is also well-supplied with household names at affordable prices. For male shoppers there is reasonably priced sportswear from Pierre Cardin, Van Heusen and Dockers.

"Our philosophy is that great design does not have to cost a lot," a Target spokeswoman told me when I was interviewing her for a newspaper story.

Thrift store chic

In South Beach, I met a makeup artist—Sunshine Harmon—with the same philosophy. Sunshine, a wife and mother of two young boys, finds bargains at Flamingo Plaza, a discount shopping center in the Miami area. "It's like a little strip mall of secondhand stores," she told me. Sunshine, formerly from the Midwest, purchased a pair of secondhand black slacks (originally from Banana Republic) for $3 at a thrift mall.

Across the country, shopping centers dedicated to thrift and re-sale stores are becoming increasingly popular. (Nationally, there are about 15,000 thrift and resale shops.) For decades antique stores—the upscale cousins of thrift stores—have teamed up to form antique shopping centers and districts, said Adele Meyer, executive director of the National Association of Resale and Thrift Shops (NARTS). That one-stop shopping concept is becoming increasingly popular with thrift stores.

"Consumers will drive further if they have more than one store to visit," Meyer said. "I'm seeing more of it happen." On its website, *www.NARTS.org*, the trade association offers a shopping guide of stores for consumers based on zip codes.

But is it possible to shop at Salvation Army, Goodwill and independent thrift stores, and still look like something that stepped off the glossy pages of an upscale fashion magazine? I found answers to that question in the November 2006 issue of *GQ* magazine. My favorite piece was a savvy and surprisingly frugal article called "The Art of Wearing Vintage," as featured in The Sartorialist column. The article features fashion maven Derrick Miller, creative director of New York-based Barker Black Shoes. The Sartorialist (*www.thesartorialist.com*) is "shocked" that Miller wears vintage (translation: thrift-store garments) but always looks as if his outfits are "tailor-made for him."

Thrift store tips from the Male Fashion Maven

1. Avoid vintage stores, which are usually overpriced, Miller said. He loves going to the Salvation Army in upscale neighborhoods, even when he's on vacation.

2. Shop for quality fabrics.

3. Don't obsess about labels. If something is ugly or looks terrible on you, a fashionable, trendy or expensive label will not change that harsh fact. Put the ugly thing back.

4. Fondle the sweaters. "If you're hunting for sweaters, this is the one time it pays to touch every piece in the store," according to a quote from Miller in the article.

5. Obsess about buttonholes and shirt-patterns. Make sure buttonholes work and are not frayed. Seek out shirt patterns you like.

6. Socks and underwear. Don"t buy used socks and underwear!

Even Hollywood goes frugal

A number of frugal fashion choices help to create the style scene at *Desperate Housewives*. In addition to a few eye-popping expensive accessories and gear, the stylists for the hit show also hit the racks at Claire's and other low-cost stores.

Cate Adair, the show's costume designer, has described her professional shopping habits this way: "Everywhere and anywhere. Swap meets, secondhand shops, boutiques, little shops, big shops, some designer labels. We'll buy stuff at the Gap."

Wearing my professional hat as a newspaper reporter, I've found great bargains on the Internet. My finds include prom dresses for $1 and trendy skirts (originally sporting triple-digit prices) for $25 to $45. A little while ago, I purchased a cute pink skirt on eBay for $8.99, plus

$5 for shipping and handling. With a very cute sweater ($6.49 from Target) and handmade Italian shoes (on sale from Marshalls), I've worn my pretty little skirt to two dress-up parties so far and have received lots of compliments.

The Frugal Duchess' Online Shopping Guide

Take stock. Know your measurements; know what you need. To buy a skirt, you should know the width of your waist and hips, and the length of your legs, especially from waist to knee. On an earlier purchase, I wasted money after buying a secondhand Gap skirt for $4.99, plus shipping. The skirt was too short. A bargain is not a bargain if the garment doesn't fit or if it matches nada in my closet. I also save time and money by shopping for fashion trends in print and online magazines.

Narrow your search. On eBay and *Amazon.com*, you can search by brand name, designer or retailer. Or you can search by description, such as: Pink Tulle Skirt. Decide if you want an item that is "new with tags" (NWT), "almost new," or "gently worn." You can search for least expensive, most expensive or quick-ending auctions.

Research the seller. Many online markets work with retailers (private sellers and major chains). Read customer comments and ratings. The feedback is often brutally frank and helpful.

Scrutinize shipping and handling fees. A $1 skirt is not a bargain if shipping and handling fees are outrageous. You're better off at a hometown discount chain.

There are several online shopping portals that compare vendor/retail prices at a variety of outlets, *www.Shopzilla.com*, *www.PriceRunner.com*, *www.Shopping.com*, *www.Pricegrabber.com* and *www.NexTag.com*. Those services are helpful for researching the best deals over the Internet and comparing them to traditional brick-and-mortar deals you find when you go out shopping. FD

Spam 'n Eggs
for Breakfast

I fantasize about making pots of soup in my Dream House, where the kitchen sports wood cabinets, marble countertops, Kohler fixtures and Thermador appliances. There's even an island in the center of the mosaic tile floor, where I could chop celery, carrots, and potatoes for my frugal soups, which are less than 15 cents a serving.

Surprisingly, the kitchen in the Mediterranean is small—just a drop larger than the one in my apartment. Such a tiny, albeit, glitzy kitchen in a big house intrigues me, and I have cooked up a few theories.

Maybe back in 1934, the Mediterranean was built as a modest vacation home for seasonal residents—Wealthy Florida Snowbirds—whose itinerary included subtropical winter getaways and restaurant meals. In that scenario—even during the Depression—home-cooked meals were not on the menu.

Or perhaps, when the Mediterranean was later expanded and remodeled during the go-go 1980s or the hot-dot-com era of the late 1990s, the kitchen retained its original Depression-era size because frugal stay-at-home meals had become quaint, but out-dated notions. Why cook when South Beach beckoned with Cuban, Sushi, Thai, French and Nouvelle Cuisine eateries?

I'm not sure. But I do know that the tiny kitchen in my Dream House is the only room in that massive house that makes me appreciate my apartment. Inch for inch, even with all of the fancy appliances, the kitchen in the Mediterranean represents just another island for making soup.

And on that island I remember how fortunate I am to live in a spacious three-bedroom apartment with shiny white tile floors and a view (from a few blocks away) of the Atlantic Ocean. I have lived in my rented corner of paradise for most of my married life. And on my waterfront island, I remember that I have been blessed to begin married life with my own kitchen. Not everyone is that lucky.

Spam and Tofu and a Dream House

When my parents were first married in August of 1957, a year before I was born, they didn't have a kitchen. At the time they were undergraduates at Cheyney State College, a small Black teachers college about 60 miles outside of Philadelphia.

After the wedding, they moved off campus to Nicetown, a quaint neighborhood in North Philadelphia. "Nicetown was named for a group of Dutch Huguenots, who around 1700 settled near what is now Hunting Park Avenue," according to records from the Free Public Library in Philadelphia.

These days, many of the townhouses in Nicetown are considered "architecturally and historically significant homes." But when my parents lived in Nicetown it was simply a "nice neighborhood." in North Philadelphia, a section of town filled with Black working-class families that had moved from southern states.

My mother has fond memories of Nicetown.

"All of the houses were in a little row. They each had a flower box. The neighborhood even had a homeowners association," my mom said.

In Nicetown, my parents rented space in a modest row house owned by a husband-wife team of domestics. My mother met them during her weekend work as a nanny. They all worked for the same family, and for a small monthly fee, the older couple provided my parents with a few rooms.

As part of the deal, my mother shared the landlords' kitchen. My mother—a brilliant student, who would later enroll in a doctorate program—was not yet a good cook and often burned food in her landlords' pristine kitchen. My mother's cooking became a bone of contention between the newlyweds and their live-in landlords.

Therefore, because of limited skills, finances and cooking space, my parents dined on a very restricted menu. They often had Spam 'n eggs for breakfast, Spam sandwiches for lunch and Spam mixed with baked beans or canned green beans for dinner. Occasionally, peanut butter and jelly sandwiches provided a taste of variety. Decades later, my folks take great pleasure in deleting spam from their computer email files, and they've completely deleted the canned processed meat from their diet. My folks—usually very frugal—love to dine out, and I blame it on Spam.

"We don't eat Spam because we had it every kind of way," my mother recently told me.

I remember Spam. It wasn't often, but when money was tight, Spam-pink meat that tasted and looked like pencil erasers appeared on our dinner table. To my childhood taste buds, Spam was napkin food: 1) chew it; 2) cough it into a paper napkin; and 3) toss it. We ate Spam during the years before and after my parents moved into their Dream House in the suburbs. That custom-built, split-level home was built on Spam.

Tofu—processed, organic bean curd—is the new Spam in my house. My husband and I serve tofu grilled with Tamari, tofu with eggs, and tofu with stir-fried vegetables. We even dice it up and serve tofu in soups, where it floats like chicken. We purchase organic tofu from a national health food chain in our neighborhood, and even our local supermarket sells tofu.

Like my mother's use of Spam, our tofu creativity seems boundless: It's great with eggs and even as a ricotta cheese substitute in lasagna. We've tossed chunks of tofu into the blender with fresh garlic, olive oil, lemon juice, and herbs and called it a dip. We have even dressed up tofu to look like slices of Gefilte (white) fish at formal meals. We call it Ge-fake-a fish and laugh. But secretly, I worry that one day my kids will exchange horror stories about tofu-and-eggs. And as I open packages of tofu, I wonder how much Spam my parents ate before they bought their dream house.

My husband and I have many strategies for cutting our grocery bill. With a little effort we reduce our annual grocery bills by thousands of dollars. Our strategies include knowing pricing trends at local supermarkets, careful use of coupons, bulk purchases and delayed gratification.

It's also possible to call food manufacturers for pricing insights. One pasta maker, for example, told a friend of mine which local retailers sold the company's pasta products at the lowest prices.

Price Zones. Even within the same supermarket chain, prices for individual products often vary greatly. For example, my mother, who now lives in Central Florida, has spotted a range of prices for the same item at different Publix locations. Friends and readers have also noted sharp price differences between two branches of the same chain. That's because many chains zone their prices according to zip codes based on the local cost of real estate, labor and other operations at each store. You can find the lowest prices by either shopping around or checking the company's website, where weekly specials are available for different stores based on zip code or neighborhood.

Create Your Own Snacks. If you don't have time to shop for deals, there are other cost-cutting strategies. A family of four can save $2,000 to $3,000 a year by skipping individually-packaged food items in favor of jumbo-sized boxes and packaging their own food in reusable items, according to Earth 911, a nonprofit group based in Arizona. Earth 911 calculates that paper towels and napkins cost more than $260 a year for a family of four. Other budget busters include disposable cups, razors and many other one-time use products.

Raisins are a perfect example of potential savings, according to Meryl Klein, the Gainesville-based director of outreach for Earth 911 (*www.earth911.org*). Shoppers can save "tremendously" by purchasing large containers of raisins and then making individual servings. Many re-usable/re-sealable containers are perfect for lunchboxes or day-trips.

Time Savers. Individual servings of cereal, juice, bottled water and dried fruit are expensive. Prepackaged individual servings of snacks and lunchbox goodies cost up to 300 percent more per ounce than larger packages of the same item, according to the editors of *Shameless Shortcuts: 1,027 Tips and Techniques That Help You Save Time, Save Money, and Save Work Every Day*. Of course, prepackaged items do speed up lunch chores. But with planning, you can "single serve yourself," and also save time and money, according to *Shameless Shortcuts*.

Here's the drill: As soon as you get home from the grocery store, divide large packages of raisins, chips and other snacks into individual-size portions in airtight containers. This organizational step provides the convenience of single servings and the cost savings of bulk purchases.

But all bets are off during family vacations, admits Earth 911's Klein. When faced with the daunting combination of children, hotels and travel arrangements, Klein finds that nothing beats the convenience of individually-packaged servings for her children. So save it for vacations! And imagine the savings of packaging things yourself. You might even be able to afford to go on that vacation!

Checking Out The Grocery Game

Just imagine $482 extra in your monthly budget. That's the average grocery savings (for a family of four) with "Teri's List." Available on the Internet, "Teri's List" is part of The Grocery Game, a weekly shopping list of savings. It's a fee-based service that provides specials in your zip code.

Launched in early 2000 by Teri Gault, a stay-at-home mom, The Grocery Game has developed a national following, now covering all 50 states. Recently featured on the CBS Early Show, Gault is also frequently quoted in many national magazines.

Available at The Grocery Game (*www.thegrocerygame.com*), the service works like this: Registered site members log on for a weekly list of savings in their neighborhood. Armed with regionalized lists of the best discounts, shoppers can save time and money. What's more, by combining savings with coupons, your potential savings are even greater. I spoke to Teri and she gave me these tips:

Stockpile. Build your own store. Buy more than you need at rock-bottom prices.

Think small. When combined with coupons, a weekly special in a small package may yield larger savings (relative to a jumbo package) on a per-unit basis.

Don't ignore convenience dinners. Most people opt for take-out food or restaurant meals because of time constraints and the hurried pace of modern life. For those no-time-to-cook meals, Teri recommends frozen dinners.

Review the math. As a weekly special, frozen dinners ($1.50 to $2 each) cost less than $10 for four. Comparable restaurant meals would cost $40 to $50. So stock up and save the frozen dinners as a restaurant alternative. Urban singles are more likely to eat out. Therefore, a stockpile of discounted frozen meals will dramatically reduce expenses.

Organic food for less

And if you want home-cooked food with the flavor of an expensive restaurant, try organic produce. Chefs at some high-end restaurants prefer to whip up their culinary treats with the vivid flavors provided by organic produce. And many organic products are tastier and healthier than their conventional counterparts.

Unfortunately for those of us on a tight budget, hefty price tags often put organic foods out of reach. But you don't have to carve up your budget to serve organic produce and food, said Craig Minowa, an environmental scientist with the Organic Consumers Association, a nonprofit industry group.

"There are multiple techniques for saving dollars when buying organic," Minowa said.

His first tip is familiar to thrifty shoppers. Use coupons and store specials to pick up organic items. Like their industry counterparts, health food stores have weekly specials and other promotions. By combining coupons with weekly specials, it's possible to purchase organic products at reasonable prices.

Buying in bulk or special ordering a large shipment of a specific item is also a frugal alternative. Many food cooperatives and health food stores will accept bulk or special order purchases from consumers, Minowa said. And don't forget standard channels. Conventional supermarkets also offer periodic sales on organic produce and organic products at bulk rate prices are also available at big box outlets such as Costco.

You can also start your own buying club or food co-op with friends and neighbors, Minowa said. To take this route, he recommends several steps: establish a monthly meeting; draw up a group shopping list; and research buying channels. Your club can either make bulk purchases through an existing food co-op or establish direct connections with different organic food distributors.

You can also go straight to the source by tapping into the network of organic farmers associated with the Community Supported Agriculture (CSA) system. Across the country, there are about 1,000 farmers enrolled in CSA. At varying rates, consumers pay a membership fee to a CSA farm and for that fee, receive direct shipments of organic farm products. It's like buying a stock or ownership share in a company.

The U.S. Department of Agriculture provides information about CSA farms throughout the country at the Alternative Farming Systems Information Center (*www.nal.usda.gov/afsic/pubs/csa/csa.shtml*). You can use the USDA database to locate a CSA farm in your zip code and you can also find local CSA listings by tapping into Local Harvest (*www.localharvest.org*). The website has links to other non-profits and government information about organic food.

Organic food clubs

For over a year, I've been a member of an organic food club. As part of the club, I buy organic produce for about 20 percent below retail prices, and the discount is even higher during peak harvest periods, according to our club organizer. There are organic buying clubs all are over the country. The co-op in my neighborhood works like this:

1. We pay a $43 fee every two weeks. That fee represents our share in the co-op. Members that help with the distribution, bagging and weighing of vegetables and produce receive extra food or additional perks.

2. Our membership share entitles us to a bi-weekly shipment of two grocery bags full of fruits and veggies. We purchase other items as needed.

3. We pick up the organic produce from a designated location (a community building or the home of a hosting member). The pickup site is convenient, typically within a five-minute drive from our home, which roughly equals our commute to the grocery store.

4. Our produce is bagged in cloth canvas bags that are re-used from week to week. We bring in one set of empty canvas bags and receive another set that is fully stocked. When we forget our bags, paper is used, but this substitution is not encouraged.

Water as budget buster

For sure, bottled water was not on the shopping list when my parents were newlyweds. More recently, due to health and fitness concerns, it's become trendy to stock up on bottled water. But believe it or not, bottled water may not be the safest option for you and your family, according to report from the University of Florida (Pinellas County Extension):

"Sales of bottled water in this country have exploded in recent years. Bottled water, in spite of its popularity, may not be safer or more healthful than tap water. Some studies have found that tap water tends to have lower bacterial counts than bottled," the report said, adding: "Also, some brands are just packaged municipal tap water, sometimes further treated, sometimes not. In addition, bottled water is costly and bulky. Thick opaque containers can impart a plastic flavor. Big, rigid polycarbonate water-cooler jugs can leave chemical residues."

In 2007 it was discovered and subsequently released through the media that a number of regional and national companies—including Aquafina and Dasani—sell refiltered tap water and call it "purified drinking water" on the label.

Aquafina, for example, sells refiltered municipal water from approximately 34 municipalities throughout the country, according to a consumer service representative for that company. The water is filtered through a three-step process that removes 98 percent of all "total dissolved solids," the customer rep told me. Keep in mind that, under federal law, municipal water quality is monitored more frequently than bottled water.

Of course, filtering your own water—with a home system—is the cheapest solution. One industry source estimates that *home-filtered water* costs three cents a gallon, compared to $1 a gallon and higher for bottled water.

The economics are compelling. At a store, bottled water can cost 89 cents to $2 a gallon, according to *Consumer Reports*. Various vendors of home filtering systems claim their products can filter your water at prices ranging from 3 cents to 18 cents a gallon. *Consumer Reports*, however, has tested 19 models and estimates that home-filtered water can cost 30 to 50 cents a gallon.

Companies such as BRITA Products and Culligan International offer a variety of high-tech and low-tech products. For roughly $20, BRITA and Culligan sell filtering pitchers. These pitchers operate quite simply. Tap water is poured into the upper chamber of the pitcher, dripped through a filter and directed into the lower portion. This is an affordable way to filter and store drinking water in your home, based on the laboratory tests run by *Consumer Reports*.

However, it takes a few minutes for water to run through the filter system, so it's easy to get impatient. (*Consumer Reports* estimates that it takes about 20 minutes to filter a half gallon of water.) I own a filtering pitcher and I agree with that assessment.

Other home filtering products, called "faucet mounts," can be placed directly on your kitchen tap. We have recently purchased a filter system for our kitchen faucet. It's a frugal option to bottled water. There are also a wide-range of under-the-sink filtering systems. Industry wide, under-the-sink systems start around $500 with installation. But that investment adds to the value of your home and can save you money, according to one industry source. ꟼᗡ

Evicted From Paradise

urnt Spam and other crispy treats led to the eviction of my parents from Nicetown, the first home of their married life, in the fall of 1957. Their landlord—who was meticulous about the shared kitchen—was fed up with my mother's burned food. My dad—then a college student at day and a grocery store employee at night—now laughs when he tells the story. But it wasn't funny at the time.

"I came home from work. It was close to midnight and your mom and the landlords were arguing. She had burned some food and had smoked up the place," my father told me laughing.

But even through the laughter, I hear the serious message in my father's stories: Be prepared for unexpected events, such as emergencies, hostile landlords, burnt food and evictions. And he's right.

Unfortunately, early in our marriage, my husband and I also learned the importance of emergency planning and tight rental agreements. Like my parents, we had an informal rental agreement with a home-owner and almost overnight, we were also evicted from our first home in the South Beach area of Miami.

Our rental of a large Art Deco house provided us with two bedrooms, our own kitchen, a fabulous 1940s-era circular dining room and a backyard filled with mango, fig, and kumquat trees. After living in the Northeast, with its frost-bitten winters, I thought we had re-discovered the Garden of Eden. For $800 a month—a real bargain compared to our New York apartment ($1,180 for three rooms)—we leased one half of the house and our landlord lived in the other half. We sealed the deal with warm wishes and a handshake, but no formal rental agreement. What a mistake!

Like Adam and Eve, we were quickly evicted from paradise after our landlord—dazzled by South Beach dollars—quietly put his property on the market in the fall of 1993. At that time, real estate prices in South Florida were just beginning to take off. We discovered our pending eviction when perspective buyers showed up for an Open House tour. Instantly, we became tour guides and evicted tenants. As such, we were just one of the many displaced victims of the booming South Beach real estate market.

Therefore only months after moving from New York, my husband I faced another set of moving costs. We needed large checks to cover the fees and deposits required to enter a standard lease agreement in the apartment building in which we now live. We learned fast that for emergencies like that and others, it's important to have an emergency fund.

Cracks in our nest eggs

Although it's important to save and build nest eggs and emergency funds, the nuts and bolts of life often throw a monkey wrench into those plans to save.

"Surprisingly, those ages 35-44—a group with high earning potential—had the hardest time building a nest egg due to debt," according to A.G. Edwards, an investment and money management firm, which created the Nest Egg Score Survey. Here are a few of the firm's findings:

♦ Forty-seven percent of survey participants believe that building a nest egg is "Essential or extremely important."

♦ Fifty-five percent rated daily expenses and cost of living as the largest savings hurdle.

♦ Twenty-eight percent said they had too much debt to save.

Emergency Fund Sources

Most experts recommend a target of three to six months of your salary or expenses. I've been brainstorming for painless and practical methods to beef up my emergency fund.

Sell your stuff

With a prudent eye and a little time, your closets, garage and deep storage areas could yield valuable merchandise for resale. "It's almost like a second source of income," said Lynn Rachel Garber, owner of Rachel's Rare Finds, a secondhand store in South Florida.

Nationwide, consignment stores typically pay the consignee 40 percent to 60 percent of the selling price. Other stores—called "resale shops"—will buy furniture and clothing directly from owners and then place those items for sale.

"It certainly is a wonderful way for people to turn their clutter into cash," said Adele Meyer, executive director of the National Association of Resale & Thrifts Shops (NARTS), an industry trade group. "Resale is the ultimate in recycling."

If you're looking to cash in on this market, NARTS has suggestions for reselling merchandise through consignment and resale stores:

1. Carefully evaluate consignment and resale stores. Ask about store policies, commissions, payment schedules and customer base.

2. Become familiar with seasonal trends in merchandise.

3. Make your merchandise look appealing. Clothing should look and

smell clean. Furniture should be polished and dusted. Make small repairs to enhance the value of the item.

4. Stay in contact with the shop and keep a list of items that have been placed for consignment.

Tapping into a second income

Second jobs, freelance assignments, and overtime hours are also options for building savings. For instance, on the streets of Miami Beach, I recently spotted a neighbor (in her 20s) wearing a Dippin' Dots uniform while walking her dog. I was puzzled by the ice cream store uniform.

"I thought you worked in a doctor"s office," I asked her.

"Still there. Dippin' Dots is my part-time job," she explained.

She works a second job in order to pay off a student loan and auto debt. She lets about three months of extra paychecks accumulate in a special savings account and then applies the lump sum to her student loan balance. It's easier, she said, to see progress with this strategy. Likewise, my dad used these strategies to make his second job work:

Keep track of the uniform. Many second jobs involve a uniform or some kind of dress code that is very different from our 9-to-5 wardrobes. My dad kept his waiter's uniform in the car or in his locker during the school week. This strategy made it easier for him to make a quick change with minimal effort. Time was a precious commodity because after the school bell rang, my dad worked until midnight several days a week.

Plan your time wisely. Arrive at the second job a little early. Getting to work ahead of time provides time to freshen up, change and relax between shifts.

Remain focused on financial goals. Working a second job is easier if you constantly remember your financial goals, such as paying off debt or saving for a house, my dad said.

The extra job "was just something that had to be done," he said. "I was just determined and put my mind to it."

Take care of yourself. "You must mentally prepare yourself and get as much rest as you can," my dad said.

Managing that extra paycheck is key

Save the part-time pay in a separate account. This keeps the extra paycheck from disappearing. The accumulated savings builds momentum, which makes it easier to save. The money feeds itself.

Pay bills. Extra paychecks can be used to pay specific monthly bills.

Cover emergencies. Spare funds are valuable for paying unexpected car repairs, medical expenses or other one-time costs.

Buy household items. Replacing our shrinking supply of silverware was low on my priority list, but we really needed a new set. Therefore, I used a second-source income check to purchase a new set of flatware from an online vendor. Because the replacement set did not come out of our normal budget, the silverware felt like a free gift when it arrived via UPS.

In addition to the extra paychecks, there are other perks to part-time employment, according to *Careerbuilder.com*.

- ♦ Free tickets to cultural events (ushers for plays, cinemas and museums).

- ♦ Discount passes for theme parks or exhibits.

- ♦ Employee shopping discounts: (bookstores, clothing stores and other specialty retailers).

- ♦ Free food. Waiters and employees of catering firms, cafes and restaurants often get free meals.

- ♦ Mentors. I've learned a lot from co-workers at my various part-time jobs.

- ♦ Career advancement. I know of one bank executive, who began her career as a part-time receptionist during her college years. The contacts and knowledge that she acquired during her part-time stint led to a full-time, high-powered career move.

- ♦ Enhanced time management skills. Anyone who works part-time while working or studying full time becomes well-schooled on the ABCs of time management.

♦ New skills. My son picked up extra organizational skills while working the cash register at a local pizza shop. Likewise, my stints as a part-time waitress also taught me a lot about efficiency and focus.

♦ Appreciation. A second job really opened my eyes to the difficult tasks my parents faced while working extra hours in addition to their full-time professional careers as educators. Working along side seasoned cashiers, waitresses and clerks also made me sensitive to the financial difficulties faced by minimum wage and low-salaried employees, who work full time in stores, restaurants and other jobs. They often do a lot of work for little pay and minimal benefits.

Saving surprise money

Found money—unexpected cash—arrives in many forms. From a forgotten $20 bill discovered in a pocket to a surprise year-end merit raise, our budgets are periodically fattened with cash from unusual sources.

But not everyone uses found money prudently. Stories about rags-to-riches-to-rags lottery winners are common. Like air conditioning blowing through a top-down convertible, found money often disappear.

What is the best use for spare cash and found money? I asked Ellen Siegel, a Miami-based financial planner who has appeared on the *Nightly Business Report*. Her answers surprised me. Bottom line: Your use of spare cash depends on the size of the bonus and the health of your financial and emotional accounts.

"So much of this conversation is about emotions," Siegel said.

An honest audit of your spending habits will determine if surprise cash should be used to pay off credit-card debt or boost retirement or savings accounts. For instance, if you are a compulsive shopper or an "emotional spender"—seeking an instant feel-good lift from new merchandise—you should think twice about applying windfalls to pay down credit card-debt, Siegel said.

For undisciplined spenders, a maxed out credit-card balance effectively closes one shopping avenue, whereas a newly-liberated balance may create a new license to spend. Siegel recommends that compulsive shoppers divide windfalls between long-term savings and retirement accounts, while making monthly credit card payments.

However, if you maintain a low or zero balance, then found money is wisely applied to your outstanding credit-card balance. This strategy works well for consumers who face a credit crunch due to one-time events such as a job loss or family illness. In those situations, paying down credit-card debt, especially high-interest cards, will liberate a large portion of the monthly budget.

Meanwhile, a small bonus—such as a $25 birthday check from a relative—may fit best in your memory account, Siegel suggests. She recommends a dinner out or some other treat. "If it's small and can't make a difference, just enjoy it and create a memory," Siegel said, adding, "Or give it away."

Picking My Own Pockets: Small Changes

Like pennies from heaven, a trail of coins runs through my home. There are dimes in the desk drawer, nickels near the computer and quarters under the sofa. One day, I collected more than $15 in "pocket money" from the corners of my home. That small change could add up to large savings. There is a lot of power in pennies.

My own parents amassed a large pile of loose change for my oldest son. In honor of his Bar Mitzvah, my folks filled a large coin bank for Tali. He was surprised that the contents—nickels, quarters and dimes—held more than $250.

Loose change has additional earning power when prudently invested in stocks, bonds, mutual funds or passbook accounts. For example, in 1978, if I had invested $150 of my baby-sitting money in Federal Express that investment would be worth $17,732.14 today. That's a return of nearly 12,000 percent.

Even small amounts of capital can be invested in financial markets. Through dividend reinvestment plans—known as DRIPs—you can invest as little as $10 in individual stocks. In a DRIP plan, your dividends are automatically channeled back into additional purchases of stock.

Your funds painlessly accumulate below the radar of frivolous spending. Different publicly traded companies have a variety of options, including plans without fees.

If you think the stock market is just another form of legalized gambling, then consider a bank or a credit union. If $250 is invested in a bank account today it would be worth an additional $26 to $178 in 10 years based on current rates, according to Mark Holmes of Eastern Financial Florida Credit Union, South Florida's largest credit union.

But the difference is especially dramatic if $250 in loose change is applied to your loan balances, Holmes said. An extra payment of $250 on a $2,500 credit-card balance would save about $300, excluding the original $250 in small coins. If your spare change were applied to the $200,000 principal of a 30-year mortgage, you would save about $1,449 in interest over the life of the loan.

Fortunately, loose change—like humidity in July—is everywhere. Almost everyone has a strategy for collecting pocket change. I've heard of shoppers who constantly break larger bills and hide the change in a savings account. A federal credit union in Texas urges its customers to "empty your pockets each day and put the spare change in your home-buying account."

Other financial mavens recommend the pay-yourself luxury tax, which works like this: Make your own gourmet coffee, do your own nails or wash your own car. Save the money that you would have spent in a jar to use for emergencies or deposit it in a savings account. My parents used a variety of those strategies when they were forced to leave Nicetown. FD

The Baby Who Slept
in a Drawer

O f course, I'm in deep denial about the affordability of my $2.6 million Dream House. In my deluded, fantasy-driven mind, I really believe that one day I will own that house—which at 3,600 square feet is larger than the 2,700-square-foot, four-bedroom home owned by Paris Hilton in the Hollywood Hills of southern California.

Despite the numbers, pending ownership is so real to my family that we have had protracted battles over bedroom assignments. My husband and I have settled the arguments with this verdict: the two youngest will move into the adjoining bedrooms—linked by a shared bathroom—on the first floor. And the Junior Suite, with its own bathroom, closet and staircase on the southern corner of the second floor, will belong to my oldest son until he goes to college. Everyone has accepted that arrangement.

But honestly, the floor plan puzzles me. For example, I worry about the distance between the children's bedrooms on the south wing and the parent's master bedroom on the opposite northern-most tip of the property. And because of the layout, I can't imagine living in that house when my children were younger. I always liked being near enough to hear them cry.

Likewise, my parents held me in close corners when I was a baby. We lived in a tiny apartment on Saint Bernard Street in west Philadelphia, where my parents moved after they were evicted from Nicetown. With their networking through friends and relatives they found a new apartment. My parents' first apartment on Saint Bernard Street cost $35 a month in 1957, for a third-floor attic apartment that consisted of a bedroom and a small kitchen.

"As college students, that's what we could afford," my mom said. "When you're young, you are just happy to be in your own place."

The good news: their new apartment had a kitchen, with room for a table, a few chairs and a small stove. The bad news: there was no refrigerator. My parents, however, found a creative solution to their food storage problems. Because they relocated in November, and the weather was cold, my parents stored food outside in a box that rested on the roof of a lower floor. They literally climbed out of a window to retrieve food from their "ice box."

Not all of their friends, however, were comfortable with that cold storage solution. During one visit, a friend accepted the offer of a small snack. But when we reached out onto the roof, she said, "No thanks," my dad recalls.

The problem of no refrigerator was resolved, however, shortly before I was born in the summer of 1958. In anticipation of my arrival, my folks rented a larger apartment also on Saint Bernard Street. For $45 a month, they acquired more space and even a refrigerator. Whether or not I had a crib, however, is debatable. My mother said that I slept in a padded drawer because they didn't have a crib for me.

"We could just take the drawer out and put it by the bed," my mom said. But my dad, however, assures me that yes, indeed there was a crib and I only slept in a drawer when an aunt watched me overnight when my parents were away on a short vacation. I've listened to both versions and I hear the truth, namely: There are creative ways to furnish a home and a nursery when you are on a budget.

One South Beach mother, Sunshine Harmon, found attractive furniture and bargains at thrift stores. As an avid environmentalist, Harmon creates room in her budget for costly organic and environmentally-friendly products by shopping for clothes, furniture and accessories in secondhand stores.

Her thrift store treasures have included a three-piece sofa set for $100, and a dining room set with four chairs and a table leaf for $100 from the Salvation Army. She also shopped at Red, White and Blue (a national thrift store chain) for children's items. For $1.95, Harmon recently found a traveling high chair in great condition. Unfortunately, she had just purchased that same bright plastic chair (new) for $20 at an area chain store. She returned the new chair—still in the box—and rehabilitated its older twin. "I washed it up and my husband didn't know the difference," Harmon said.

Her thrift shopping came in handy after a costly online shopping mistake. Over the Internet, Harmon had purchased a new baby sling for $39. The item arrived in the wrong size, but was not returnable after she washed it. However, at Red, White and Blue, Harmon purchased a similar carrier in the right size for only 95 cents.

At home with hotel furniture

Hotel furniture and fixture sales are an affordable way to decorate a home or office with sofas, tables and other items. With a mixture of functional and fashionable furniture, hotel sales have become trendy, too. From chunky '50s-style couches to funky lamps, hotel redecorating sales offer a range of unusual merchandise at a great price. Due to frequent remodeling, new ownership or teardowns, many hotels offer special clearance sales. Several years ago we purchased dressers, lights and television sets for less than $25 each at a hotel in South Beach.

For example, in 2007 the Seville Beach Hotel in South Beach sold the furnishings from its rooms. Double beds sold for $40 each, dressers for $15 and black-out drapes for $10. Lamps, pictures and armchairs were $5 each. Handled by International Content Liquidations, Inc., the sale also included Art Deco "lipstick chairs," color TVs, a piano, office furniture and assorted fixtures. Shoppers included Karen Fryd, founder of the South Florida Youth Foundation. Fryd purchased furniture and fixtures for several nonprofit organizations. With assistance from teachers and volunteers, she bought a stainless steel service table and a banquet table.

"I thought the prices were phenomenal," Fryd wrote in an email. "We did great for a couple hundred bucks!"

Sales of hotel content furnishings are usually advertised in newspapers. I have also seen fliers and posters touting sales. Hotel liquidation companies often post schedules of upcoming sales on their websites.

As seen on television

The concept has been featured in magazines, too. In an article about affordable home design, the editors of *Woman's World* featured *www.hotelsurplus.com*, a California-based company that purchases and re-sells hotel furnishings.

"The tremendous competition in the hotel market generates a constant pressure on hotels to upgrade the furnishings in their properties to reflect the most current decorating trends," according to a company statement. "Therefore, a large number of hotels often liquidate relatively recent furniture on a cyclical basis."

The company's website and California warehouse is stocked with all kinds of "no-longer-needed, gently used" pieces from top-rated hotels, according to the magazine. Recent deals include Barnabey's Olde Style Armoires for $150 each, glass and pewter tables for $20, and large overstuffed chairs for $50. The company's merchandise has been featured on several television shows including HGTV's *Design On A Dime*. You can find what's for sale at *www.hotelsurplus.com*.

Spinning on the Freecycle

Imagine if everything on eBay, the global Internet-based garage sale, traded for free. Perhaps that electronic marketplace would be called "freeBay." Don't laugh. A large Internet-based giveaway does exist throughout the country. The Freecycle Network operates an Internet-based bulletin board where items—fax machines, movie tickets, pianos and other household castoffs—are offered for free on a first-come, first-serve basis.

"One person's trash can truly be another's treasure," according to the organizers of Freecycle Network (*www.freecycle.org*).

The Freecycle Network was launched in May 2003 by RISE Inc., a Tucson, Arizona, nonprofit group committed to waste reduction, recycling and other social issues. RISE created Freecycle as a way to reduce waste in Tucson. And over the last few years, membership in the program has expanded nationally and internationally. Anyone can register by going to *www.freecycle.org* and clicking on the appropriate geographical region. Curious about the local giveaways, I recently logged onto the global Freecyle site and registered for Freecycle Miami through Yahoo.

The list of available items included a playpen, a child carrier, a recliner, a hot tub, a water softener and movie tickets. A family of five from West Palm Beach offered a free General Electric washing machine that they acquired when they purchased a new home. The machine that came with the house was in good condition and did a "great job" on the family laundry. But a gift of a newer and larger machine prompted the family to give away the older one. And as a bonus, they also offered an organic watermelon from their home garden and fresh eggs.

Getting the most from used furniture

It's not wise to randomly purchase old furniture and appliances. "You want to look for quality," said David Fernan, owner of Victoria's Attic, two vintage furniture and art stores in Fort Lauderdale, Florida. There are several things to look for when selecting used, but well-made furniture.

Peek inside. According to furniture professionals, construction of drawers, for example, offer important clues about the quality and durability of a dresser, desk or china closet. On the company website (*www.popsfurniture.com*), experts at Pop's Unfinished Furniture, a California-based company, report that drawers of poorly-made furniture typically lack guides—the tracks that smoothly open and close the drawers. Fernan said drawers in better quality furniture have either wood or metal guides.

Say no to cheap shortcuts. Glue, staples and fiberboard indicate cheap construction and a shorter life-span.

Test the sofa cushions. Low-quality sofas and chairs are often made from low-density foam cushions. These pieces look good in showrooms, but sink and sag in less than two years. Well-made sofas use higher density foam that will retain its shape for years, Fernan said. Seams can be telltale. When shopping for a sofa or chair, check the cushion seams. If the seams have become flattened or if the cushion appears to sag, don't buy the piece.

Check the weave on wicker. It's often costly to repair wicker weave, so carefully consider any purchase that needs new wicker caning, say the editors of *www.RDLiving.com*, a website affiliated with *Reader's Digest*.

Avoid reupholstering. Unless you're really in love with a piece, it may be cheaper in the long run (and less of a headache) to buy a new chair rather than paying for reupholstering.

Look past the surface. A quality piece of furniture may be lurking beneath an ugly paint job, according to my husband, who has refinished several tables and cabinets. Consider repainting or refinishing used furniture as a do-it-yourself project.

Know the market. Befriend the owners and managers of secondhand and vintage stores. Learn the weekly or monthly timetable for new shipments, donations and sales.

A diverse crowd of shoppers

My living room is a secondhand furniture gallery. The room's centerpiece is a heavy, feather-stuffed couch from a luxury home on the ocean. The previous owners—according to secondhand accounts—purchased the couch, found they were allergic to the feathers, and promptly donated the item to a thrift store. Spotting the piece during a shopping trip, my husband Avi spent $200 for an almost-new couch that was probably worth thousands.

For my husband, an interior designer, thrift shopping is a passion and a profession. The walls of our home are decorated with second-hand paintings; our living space is lit by lamps from thrift stores, and our chairs provide secondhand comfort.

And we're not alone. Driven by frugality, creativity, or community spirit, the pool of thrift-store shoppers is as diverse as the furniture and knick-knacks stocked on store shelves.

Shoppers range "from interior designers to the indigent and everyone in between. They approach decorating with fun and generosity," said Heather Klinker, founder of Grubstake, a nonprofit organization and thrift store that supports underprivileged families, especially women and children.

Grubstake offers an unusual showroom of value. Past merchandise includes armoires, tables, sofas and chairs that sell for an average price of $150 to $200. On the higher end, recent sales included a black lacquered Roche-Bobois dining room table and chairs set, featuring inlaid wood base and a glass table top. Grubstake was selling the set for $2,000, which is far below the original $20,000 ticket price.

Prices drop still lower at the end of every month, when Klinker literally cleans house at Grubstake with a bargain sale. To make room for new donations, most items like tables, lamps and other merchandise are priced at $1.

At many thrift stores, merchandise is often scooped up quickly by antique dealers and interior designers. Almost daily, professional shoppers begin their hunt early and are known to make purchases quickly after delivery trucks arrive with donated items, according to several thrift store managers. (The merchandise is typically sold as antiques in a prettier setting and at a higher price.)

"We have a lot of dealers who come here," said Terry Mack, store manager of the Douglas Gardens Thrift Store in Miami. "Frequency is the key."

Scratch-and-dent savings

While sinking into a neighbor's soft leather couch, I felt a twinge of furniture envy. The couch was part of a three-piece living room set purchased new from a national chain's clearance center. At a scratch-and-dent sale, my friend updated her living room for a fraction of the standard retail cost.

Here are her tips and other suggestions for finding fine pieces for less:

Track down clearance centers. National chains operate clearance outlets featuring furniture at steep discounts. Rooms to Go (*www.roomsto go.com),* for example, has clearance outlets throughout the country, and Neiman Marcus has Last Call Centers in different states (*www.nmlast callclearancecenter.com*).

Ask about scratch-and-dent sales. Most retailers offer a discount for new merchandise that is slightly scratched or nicked. At Brands Mart a friend purchased high-end appliances (a washer and dryer) that were USA, new, but cosmetically flawed and sold at a discount. Department and electronics stores also sell floor models at mark-down prices.

Don't be afraid to bargain. The sales staff at the clearance sale accommodated a request for color substitutions in a three-piece (monotone) furniture set. The staff also agreed to a negotiated delivery price.

Think outside the retail box, recommends the editors of *www.RDLiv ing.com.* Consignment stores, estate auctions, discount price clubs (Costco, BJ's and Sam's Club), yard sales, and flea markets sell new or gently used furniture. And a mixture of new and used furniture is stocked at the Habitat for Humanity Restore, which has stores all over the country. Visit *www.habitat.org* to learn more. FD

Dining Out with
the Rockefellers

I n the summer of 1965, right after my seventh birthday, the Beatles'
movie *Help!* hit the theaters. It was the first movie I saw at the leg-
endary Esquire Theater on Broad Street in Philadelphia. I attended
the showing with my best friend Beverly and her teenage sister
Linda.

We sat in the balcony section of the large theater. Like the rest of
the crowd, we screamed as John, Paul, George and Ringo dashed
around on the screen in front of our eyes. Paul McCartney was my favorite Beatle, and I had a metal lunchbox with his picture on it.

I don't remember much of the plot, but I remember the price of our
tickets: 50 cents for an afternoon matinee. Four decades later, it's

$9.75 for a single ticket. And I hate it. Fortunately for my family, it's free to borrow movies from the public library, including recent box office hits and kiddie favorites.

But if you simply must see latest blockbuster and first-run movies (a.k.a. budget busters), I've got a great frugal option: AAA Auto Club. Yup. Various offices sell discount movie tickets to auto club members for far less than standard fares. For example, in South Florida, our local AAA Auto Club charges $5.67 for each AMC Theater movie ticket and $6.05 for Regal Cinema. And there is no minimum purchase. Go to *www.AAA.com* and plug in your zip code for movie ticket discounts in your market. The cheap tickets have to be purchased directly through the auto club. Meanwhile, Regal Cinema and AMC also sell discount tickets if you purchase a minimum of 50 tickets. You can split the cost with others or use extra tickets as gifts.

Free summer fun at the movies

When the school year ends, movie theaters are a source of cool and frugal entertainment for parents and kids. That's because during the summer Regal Cinema hosts its annual free Family Film Festival, with free mid-week, midday showings for parents and kids.

Likewise, AMC offers a comparable $1 Summer Movie Camp that benefits charity with blockbuster G- and PG-rated Hollywood movies at 10:30 a.m. every Wednesday at select AMC theaters in many markets. For more information, go to *www.amctheatres.com.*

Disney dates and Rockefeller Center

My parents also took us out to the movies when I was growing up. Disney dates were our favorite outings.

One night in the fall of 1967, M&D took us out for dinner, where we had spaghetti and meatballs from the children's menu.

After dinner, we went to a night showing—our first ever—of *Disney's Jungle Book.* I fell in love with Mowgli the beautiful man-cub with the cute smile, the floppy hair and the skin that was brown like mine. When the lights went up, my heart stayed on the screen, where I was dancing with Baloo, the bear and Bagheera, the panther. My brother,

Ben Jr., and I picked up the beat as we sang "The Bare Necessities of Life" as M&D escorted us to the red exit signs. It all seemed like magic.

If downtown Philly was magical at night, New York City was more so at any hour of the day. From the time I was six or seven, New York was on our map. Trips to New York—church excursions, PTA-sponsored chartered bus tours and family day trips—were real treats during my childhood.

We usually went to Radio City Music Hall to watch the Rockettes for their seasonal shows. Beyond the glitter and music, I was happy on the streets of New York. I loved the old men on the corners with their carts of roasted chestnuts, salt pretzels and hot dogs smothered with grilled onions, sauerkraut, and mustard. Unfortunately, we rarely bought hot dogs on the street because my mom said the vendors handled money and then touched the food without washing their hands.

We did get to eat at New York restaurants, including the old Horn & Hardart automat cafeteria where my mom and her friends purchased cups of Maxwell House coffee and ordered donuts for the kids.

Most of all, I loved Rockefeller Center in midtown Manhattan, which was the scene of one of my favorite childhood meals. While we ate our lunch, skaters in bright hats, scarves, and mittens spun around on the outdoor ice rink just outside the restaurant's window. I still remember the winter spectacle and the food we ate that day, which—to be honest—was not so good, at least for a kid.

My siblings and I ate Salisbury steak, odd-shaped potatoes and mini vegetables, which looked strange to me. Frankly, we really wanted plain old burgers and fries, which were definitely not on the menu. But I loved that meal because I got to sip cola from a tall, cool glass and watch the skaters.

The bill was astronomical, and we were definitely not Rockefellers. To make matters worse, one mom in the group had purchased a bottle of expensive perfume from an upscale store in Manhattan. So, between the perfume, the show tickets and the Salisbury steaks, there was barely enough money to purchase our train tickets back to Philadelphia. My mother was in her late 20s at the time, and since then, both she and my father have become savvier about spending, traveling and dining out.

Stay home. Save restaurants for special treats like birthdays, anniversaries or special achievements. Make home a special place by creating theme nights: Mexican night (homemade tacos); Jerusalem adventure (falafels and pitas) or Italian night (pizza, pasta and garlic bread).

Pick child-friendly restaurants. F.F.O.—finger food only—is the code word when eating out with children. Chicken fingers, burgers or pizza are safer bets than marinated chicken, wine-basted roast beef and stuffed pasta. In general, order kid-friendly food from an age-appropriate menu to avoid paying for expensive, uneaten food.

Watch the clock. Early-bird dinner specials are not just for seniors. Many restaurants offer discounts for meals ordered in the late afternoon or early evening. One of my favorite Kosher Chinese restaurants offers a great early-bird special, with hefty cost-savings. Going out for a late lunch is also a great alternative, since lunch menus tend to be much cheaper than the dinner selection.

Skip the drinks. At $2 to $3 per serving, a round of drinks can easily exceed the cost of an entree or salad. For a family of five, that's $12.50 (plus tax) for the first round of drinks. With two drinks per person, that's $25 before you've even taken a bite (believe it or not, some restaurants don't offer free refills). "Drink water," urged one reader of my blog. "They get you on the desserts and drinks. That's where they make their money."

Save calories. By skipping dessert you can save your waistline and your budget. A thrifty reader offered this calculation: A $3 scoop of ice cream at a restaurant costs as much as a gallon of ice cream at the grocery store. And if you have a few kids clamoring for ice cream, the economics can put a chill on the meal. So if you dine out, consider serving cake and ice cream at home.

Graze and nibble. Personally, my ideal meal consists of just appetizers and dessert. A combination of soup, salad, and sweet-cakes is a thrifty treat when you are either dining alone or with a spouse. Order lots of appetizers, and share meals.

View art. Many galleries have a wonderful selection of free food and goodies on opening night. Think of it this way: It's a [light] dinner and a floor show!

Volunteer. Many charities provide huge deli platters, pizza, and other treats for volunteers who help out at events, charitable dinners, and phone-a-thons. At one pledge-a-thon, a large restaurant donated a wide selection of tasty food for helpers. My boys volunteered. They enjoyed helping out and they enjoyed the food. Plus, they received community service hours for school.

Be a snob. Skip past the stuff that you can make better and cheaper at home. Why, why, why spend $10 on fancy mac and cheese when you can make a pan-full for pennies?

And always, always tip generously. The former waitress in me rebels against cheap tippers!

Number one on cutbacks

Cutting back on restaurant meals is the number one money-saving strategy cited among consumers in the U.S., according to a survey from ACNielsen, a top market research company. Next on the list of top budget cuts: slashing energy costs (electric and gas expenses), and reducing the entertainment tab.

"In the US, the enormous amount of take-out food we consume, the billions we spend on out-of-home entertainment, and [our position] as the world's largest user of energy ... may be the big budget numbers that can be reduced without too much lifestyle compromise," said Tom Markert, Chief Marketing Officer, ACNielsen.

American Idol and Frugal Dining

Frugal dining is also on the repertoire of American Idol star Taylor Hicks who chatted about his cheap dating strategies in an issue of *People* magazine. "I think cooking is a whole lot cheaper than going out," Taylor Hicks said.

When asked about impressing dates during his frugal, pre-fame days, Hicks told the magazine that "by using [his] head," he was able to impress women for less. "I have this really great southern spaghetti recipe."

Don't order pasta

Speaking of spaghetti, I have trouble ordering pasta in restaurants. I don't suffer from wheat allergies and I'm not pasta phobic. I just know better. You see, as a young professional in New York, I worked in a few Manhattan restaurants, and I know the cost of a pasta dish. Dressed up in sauce, cheese and Portobello mushrooms, noodle entrees cost less than 50 cents to make, but were sold to diners for $8 to $12 a serving. (My boss loved to brag about his pasta profits!)

One reader, a former restaurant industry professional, agreed and left me this comment on my blog: "I worked as a chef and caterer before and I can tell you that I loved it when clients wanted pasta dinners or pasta salads. I could see the money coming in. We pretty much charged the same as we would for a steak or seafood plate," he said. FD

Household Budget Cuts

What people are doing to save	U.S.	Globally
Spend less on restaurant meals	66%	44%
Cut down on electricity and gas	61%	37%
Reduce entertainment costs	60%	57%
Trim clothing budget	54%	53%
Drive less often	47%	27%
Do more shopping with coupons	46%	19%
Buy cheaper grocery brands	42%	35%
Wait to upgrade technology	41%	48%
Eliminate yearly vacation	38%	29%
Wait to replace major household objects	37%	36%
Make fewer telephone calls	24%	34%
Search for better rates: insurance, home loans, and credit cards	16%	17%
Cut back on tobacco	8%	10%
Other	7%	7%
Won't do anything	4%	4%

Source: ACNielsen

Holidays at the Harvey's

A bright red fireplace sits in the middle of my Dream House. Such a fireplace, in such a color, is an unexpected detail in subtropical Miami, where pastel colors in whimsical shades dominate landscapes and interior design.

In primary red, the Mediterranean fireplace sparks vivid memories of Santa Claus in a bright red suit. And in fact, that Miami fireplace takes me back to Northeast winters and functional fireplaces, over which my parents hung large red velvet stockings. It's quite a distance to travel on Memory Lane because I have moved so much since childhood. Geographically, I have traveled from Manhattan to Miami; religiously, I have moved from Christianity to Judaism. But I still remember the Decembers of my childhood.

The family rituals of Christmas meant a lot to my parents. Christmas meant Nat King Cole singing about chestnuts roasting over an open fire. Christmas was the smell of chocolate chip Slice 'n Bake Pillsbury cookies and the scent of a fresh pine tree in the front room. And on Christmas Eve, we'd decorate the tree with red, green, and gold balls on hooks; strings of multi-colored electric lights, and painted wooden ornaments—including the little blue moon that my parents bought when I was a baby.

The rest of the house was decorated with holiday cards taped along the stairways and around the doorframes. And if we didn't eat them all, there were also little red and white peppermint candy canes all around the house.

Everything leading up to Christmas was magic, even the Sears catalogue, which was packed with a thick toy selection. Every page had something we wanted. My brother, Ben Jr., and our little sisters, Karen and Debbie, spent hours studying the toys.

'Make a list,' mom or dad told me when I was about seven. I was in the middle bedroom and the Sears catalog was on my lap. Bengy was about five; Karen and Debbie were pre-schoolers. I took their orders as they pointed to toys on the glossy pages.

The list was for "Santa," and M&D promised to mail it off to him. "We're his helpers," they always told us with such pride. And sometimes they even took us to the North Pole at area department stores or shopping centers, where we posed for pictures on Santa's lap. Sometimes my brother cried because the old man in the red suit scared him.

Christmas morning we'd be all smiles after discovering that the Flintstone glass jelly jar of eggnog and the plate of chocolate chip cookies—snacks for Santa—were eaten and swapped for a tree full of toys. And then finally in the late afternoon, we'd get out of our PJs, slippers, and housecoats and hop into the family car for a series of visits to the rest of our extended family and friends in the Greater Philadelphia area. Huge meals and gifts exchanged were a part of the holiday ritual.

The holiday budget

Back in 1964, when I was seven-and-a-half years old, consumers spent far less on gifts during the holiday season, compared to $457.4 billion in 2006, according to the National Retail Federation.

2006 Average Holiday Budget	
Spending Target	Amount Spent
Family	$451.34
Friends	$ 85.60
Co-workers	$ 22.40
Clergy, teachers and baby-sitters	$ 44.52
Flowers	$ 18.98
Decorations	$ 46.49
Candy and food	$ 91.20
Greeting cards	$ 30.57

Recycled gifts

But what if you don't want to spend a lot? Regifting! Many of us do it. Few of us own up to it. The problem is the word itself. To my ears, "regifting" sounds shady. But there's nothing wrong with recycling gifts. Recycled gifts are great for holidays, children's birthday parties and other events.

If I don't like knitting kits, but my neighbor Joannie is a big knitter, what's wrong with re-packaging the new and unused knitting kit from Aunt Ida and giving it to Joannie? Passing along the right gifts to the right owners is good karma and very frugal. Why should a perfectly good present turn to dust in my closet simply because it's found the wrong owner? I have four rules for recycling gifts.

1. Be mindful. It's the thought that counts. Really. Mindless recycling is a waste of energy, time, and materials. Take the time to really match the right gift to the right person.

2. Check the condition. Make sure the present is in good shape. If it's all dinged up and the packaging has become very un-gently worn, then just give it to a thrift store.

79

3. Rewrap. Refreshen. Make the gift-wrapping decorations your own before passing it on.

4. Keep Track! Don't give the gift back to the original giver.

Elegant and thrifty

Some clichés are accurate. It's really the thought that counts and homemade gifts are especially appreciated during the holiday season. And great ideas for homemade gifts abound—on the Internet, in magazines and craft books. Directions for various craft projects are available at *www.familyfun.com*, where the home page offers an "Easy-to-Make Gifts" option.

Projects include a jewelry tree made from a small branch, polymer clay, paint, and glue. Other child-friendly crafts include instructions to create furry eyeglass cases and hand-colored candles, fashioned from standard white candles, watercolors, and acrylic paints.

Meanwhile, through networking with my other frugal friends in Cyberspace, I have collected other creative holiday tips. For example, Angela, aka, "The Creative Homemaker," (*www.CreativeHomemaker. blogspot.com*), told me that she has knitted scarves and made glass beaded necklaces as gifts. Other holiday gifts have included homemade appliqué tote bags filled with cookies for neighbors and friends. And for the grandparents, she has made small scrapbooks filled with pictures of her children.

"A really cool thing to do is to take a close up photo and put it into the computer," Angela told me via email. "Then use a photo editing program that has the charcoal sketch option. Print the photo out on sketching paper and trace the lines with charcoal pencils. A simple black metal frame goes great with it and usually only costs $5."

Gifts for teachers

For one teacher at our school, a group of families organized a scrapbook gift. Each family was given a blank page from an album, with instructions to fill the empty space with photos, recipes, or decorations. When the individual pages came together, the scrapbook was filled with irreplaceable records of shared moments in the classroom, dance festivals, and other school events. As a bonus, families also contributed cash for a beautiful silver candle set.

There are also many ways to select and package holiday and year-end presents for educators and classroom assistants. At one school, PTA members collect small contributions from parents and compile the funds to provide a substantial gift certificate or cash gift for each teacher, with each family signing the card. Homemade gift projects include personalized calendars that are printed from your home computer, complete with children's drawings. Other gift ideas include a mini-garden, decorated trays, a handmade storybook or scrapbook, a custom collage on a clipboard, poems, and letters.

Beyond photo albums and hand-crafted scrapbooks, the menu of affordable, yet thoughtful holiday gifts is extensive. A free gift-giving brochure called "Simplify the Holidays" is offered on New American Dream's website *www.newdream.org*.

At my house, my children have enjoyed making necklaces, pictures and cards for their teachers. From their enthusiasm, I've learned the importance of incorporating children into the gift process for teachers.

Budget-friendly holiday baskets

At prices of $50 and higher, many gift baskets are budget busters. Fortunately, it's relatively easy to assemble gift baskets filled with skin care products, high-end chocolates, or holiday trinkets. From drug stores to craft stores, the marketplace is filled with empty containers and baskets at low prices. At one sale during the holidays, for example, the entire basket collection was half off at Michaels, a chain of craft stores.

And beyond baskets, there are other containers. An empty pot stuffed with garden gloves, seed packets, and small tools can be bundled together as a holiday package for a gardener. Theme baskets make the gift even more personal for your recipient.

Consider packaging a mixing bowl packed with freshly-baked cookies, recipes and assorted kitchen tools, or a large clear cosmetic bag stuffed with body creams, elaborate soaps and other day spa treats. Discount retail chains such as Marshalls, Ross Stores and other specialty stores also feature rotating sales of chocolates, wines, cheeses, and other gourmet treats that are perfect for holiday baskets. Just add the cellophane and the bow.

Day-after Thanksgiving shopping in August!

December shopping before Labor Day? Does that sound absurd? Actually, some of my frugal friends love to do their winter holiday shopping during the summer months. Lulu, for example, likes to save money by shopping year-round for presents. In that fashion, she can stretch out her holiday budget and purchase gifts as the mood and the price move her.

Lulu stockpiles gifts in the garage or a closet and really, really tries to focus on finding the right gift for each person on her list. Back-to-school promotions—especially with the tax holidays in different states—represent a great time to pick up trinkets, clothes, and paper goods for less, Lulu said.

Sally, a fellow blogger at Through a Glass Darkly (*www.danand sally.com*) agrees: "I love shopping for gifts year-round. It spreads the joy of planning for other people's joy around the year and keeps me from panicking about what to get people in December."

Spreading the wealth

Holiday deals and frugal shopping are gift-wrapped opportunities to give to the less fortunate. And even if your holiday budget is tight, there are painless ways to contribute to seasonal charities. By tapping into sales and assorted promotions, it's possible to satisfy gift list demands, while still giving a bundle to homeless and impoverished families. Donations of merchandise, time, and services are also appreciated at nursing homes, shelters, and other non-profit institutions. But you don't have to spend a lot to give a fortune during the holiday season.

Buy-One-Give-One-Away. For instance, buy-one-get-one (BOGO) free offers provide a frugal outlet for charitable giving. From shoes to office equipment, holiday catalogs, and shopping flyers bulge with two-for-one deals or other discounts for multiple purchases.

Toys 'R' Us, Walgreens, Office Depot, and others retailers market assorted BOGO offers, which include either free or half-off deals on merchandise. Likewise, one year educational wooden puzzles were three-for-

$10 at Target. Other retailers touted attractive specials on board games, electronic toys and other gadgets. Buy one for your gift list and donate the free or discounted items to a toy drive, a charitable thrift store or a homeless shelter.

The idea is not my own. I was inspired by my friend, Beth, a frugal shopper who picked up great deals after Halloween and donated a significant portion of her merchandise, including tissue boxes priced at 19 cents each, to a local food bank.

Community service projects

I know of other families who incorporate community service into their holiday traditions. Family or group projects include distributing baked goods at a nursing home, visiting hospital patients or serving holiday meals at a soup kitchen. Such activities not only spread good will, but provide parents with a hands-on opportunity to share the values of compassion and community service with children.

I have also heard of families and individuals who operate with a one-in, one-out system that works like this: For every new item (toy, game, or garment) received, a comparable item from the closet is donated to a thrift store or given away. On an organizational basis, this system reduces the glut of toys and trinkets after birthdays and holidays. But more, importantly, recycled merchandise—in good condition—is valuable. ⚘

Saving Money in the Suburbs

I was 39 years old and pregnant with my third child when I broke my very first bone. While literally running late for the bus to work, I landed with force on the outer edge of my left foot in downtown Miami. With a bone protruding from my foot, I was taken to the emergency room. That was a long trip from the safety of my childhood.

When I was little, other kids in other families broke bones and made repeat visits to the emergency room. But that didn't happen in our house, where my parents guarded us with watchful eyes.

For example, during the 1960s, my parents strapped the four of us into seat belts in the back seat of our white Rambler long before such procedures were required by law. We were dressed in hats, gloves, scarves, galoshes and snowsuits at any temperature below 45 degrees. And if we sneezed, M&D were on the phone with a doctor, ASAP.

Given the importance my parents placed on security, it's understandable that they were alarmed when our sleepy West Oak Lane neighborhood in north Philadelphia began to change in the mid-1960s. We had moved to that neighborhood when my parents had saved enough money for a down payment on a three-bedroom house—their first home. They needed the extra space to accommodate their growing family which included my three siblings and me. With pride, an FHA loan and a 5 percent down payment, my folks purchased their starter home for $10,500 on West Oak Lane.

We moved from our previous house after the atmosphere of our neighborhood changed as a result of the social, political and economical turmoil from the 1960s. Graffiti, street gang violence, and other signs of deterioration were muted, but still evident on our comfortable street.

Finding a new home was not easy. As a child, I remember taking long drives to look at a series of suburban ranch homes that were quickly not-for-sale when my family stepped out of our car. Real estate agents smiled nervously and home sellers quickly ended discussions when they discovered we were Black. Many times, we never walked beyond the curb or sidewalk.

Life in the suburbs

Undaunted, my parents decided to build their own home in Cherry Hill, New Jersey, in a new community built on old farmland. New green lawns were made from fresh squares of sod cut with the precision of postage stamps. The developer planted small cherry trees along the main street and provided the community with names such as Knollwood, Kingston Estates, and Windsor Park, where we lived.

Our house was on a small street called Orchid Lane. We lived in a split-level home with four bedrooms and three bathrooms, which my parents purchased for $28,000 in 1967. This was the Dream House funded by the magical earnings from the winning sweepstakes ticket and overtime pay.

Beginning in the second grade, I watched that house grow from a hole in the ground—and I didn't believe that pit was going to be a house. But when I was eight, in early 1967, we moved into our home on a hill. A tiny pear tree stood on our front lawn.

My parents loved entertaining in their new suburban home, which had a gas grill, a green and white swing set and a volleyball net in the backyard. That setting was perfect for long holiday-weekend barbecues where my parents hosted relatives, colleagues and friends from the greater Philadelphia area. Our guests drove over the Benjamin Franklin Bridge, down Route 38 and past the Garden State Race Track to our development, where my father cooked on the grill in our backyard.

We ate between fierce volleyball games and competitive horseshoe matches in the backyard. And sometimes, my dad set up the croquet brackets on the side lawn on the Fourth of July. After dark on that holiday, we all piled into cars and drove to the Garden State Race Track for the annual fireworks display, which always seemed perfect. Staring up at the dark sky, the world was a burst of bright color exploding over my head with a bang.

For years, we were the only African-American family on our block, but in many ways our little suburban enclave was a snapshot of diversity and hyphenated backgrounds.

The Chinese-American family down the hill taught us to count to five in Cantonese and to feast on pickled, salted plums.

The Greek-American family up the block invited us to their restaurant—Olga's Diner—on Route 70, and on some Saturday afternoons, my dad sipped frosted bottles of Bud beer with the father of 10 kids from the Irish-Catholic family at the top of our street.

The Italian-American family invited us to their elaborate and festive parties. And my best friend on the block was Miriam, (Mimi) a tomboy from a family of German-American Jews. Mimi's mom was from the South and spoke Hebrew with a thick Southern accent.

Of course, there were racial issues. During Ring Around the Rosie and other circle games, some children refused to hold my little sisters' hands. Others—at school or in the playground—called my brother the dreaded n-word, and at one neighborhood get-together, another homeowner casually told my father that maybe our family would be more happy with "our own kind."

But while many areas of the country became violent battle grounds for desegregation, busing, and equality, our corner of Suburbia quietly digested diversity through kickball games, lemonade stands and freeze-tag. Our neighborhood friends were permanent fixtures on the green-and-white swing set that my father installed in our backyard.

Gardening in the suburbs

My childhood in the suburbs was filled with low-cost and no-cost activities with my family and neighbors. Gardening was an activity that we enjoyed in our new suburban home. In the backyard, my father—the son of a Virginia tomato farmer—planted Jersey tomatoes, cucumbers and other vegetables. In the front yard, he created a flower bed with rose bushes, pansies and other annual flowers.

Of the four Harvey kids, my sister Karen inherited my father's green thumb. As a child, she planted and nurtured a huge sunflower plant that grew taller than her. To this day my sister enjoys a heavy harvest from her organic garden in her Central Florida backyard. A recent crop included lettuce, peppers, cherry tomatoes, collard greens, and cucumbers.

My garden—on my seventh-floor balcony—is much, much smaller than the dream home of my childhood or my Dream House of my adult years. Yet, our garden is also a retreat and serves as an outdoor room for our apartment, where my husband Avi has created a tropical landscape on a very low budget.

Gardening on the cheap

My husband's secret garden tools: unconventional containers, statues, and wrought iron furniture picked up at yard sales, junk stores and thrift shops. With an eye for color and a dream of garden delights, Avi picks up plants from Home Depot for less than $1 each and travels to nurseries that offer affordable plants and flowers. He even throws in a few edible herbs and flowers to spice up dinner-time preparations.

"There's a whole lot that can be done with very simple, very inexpensive plants," said Avi, who has purchased small pots of flowers for as little as 88 cents.

The flowers—featuring a riot of purple petunias, passion fruit flowers, and pink snapdragons—add color to the balcony greenery. But unusual containers and accents really make the garden come alive. For instance, an old wrought iron table—purchased for about $10 at a thrift store—now serves as an unusual plant stand against the southern wall of our balcony.

Unusual wastepaper baskets, small tin baths and even the utilitarian black plant tubs are also options for affordable and interesting garden containers. Dollar stores yield a few surprises for the garden, including wind chimes. What's more, discarded statues, old signs, sculptures and birdhouses are available at thrift stores throughout our area. My husband recently found a small resin birdhouse for $1 and a small pot decorated with a delicate fairy for $2. With a touch of paint, a dash of tolerance and a creative flair, rejects from another household can accent a patio or garden.

Our children, of course, are our best garden ingredient. Their delight in picking fresh herbs for omelets or flowers for the table is priceless.

Cheap plants are everywhere

There are many sources for free or cheap greenery. Plenty of plants and pots from garage sales decorate my porch garden. In addition to yard sales, there are many sources of either inexpensive or free sources of plants and flowers, said Sue Williams of *www.frugalgardening.com*.

William's number one tip? "Never be afraid to ask for anything," she said. Working as an activities director for a nursing home and as a foster parent, Williams said she "always needed help getting supplies for both jobs. Consequently, I learned to ask for what I wanted as well as what I needed. I discovered people are very willing to help and to share. They just need to be asked."

Online sources of free plants include *www.Freecycle.org* and *www.CraigsList.org*. Online communities that feature free or low-cost merchandise are good sources of free plants. Williams recommends posting an online notice requesting excess plants from gardeners.

◆ Friends and co-workers are a great source. Many offices include a number of expert gardeners. One year, for example, I grew a wide variety of specialty tomatoes thanks to a co-worker who brought in small samples from his garden. He also gifted my garden with a small passion fruit flower vine and herbs. More importantly, his plant expertise was valuable.

◆ Ask the professionals. Believe it or not, plant nurseries can be an "excellent" source of free plants, Williams said. She has received freebies by asking nurseries for plants that have not sold and may be discarded. Likewise, *landscaping crews* often discard older plants when updating a garden. Williams has asked road crews for plants are that headed for the trash bin or the compost pile. She has even used the Yellow Pages to hunt for landscaping crews willing to donate discarded plants. Caution: Your free plants may not look like much during the first year, but with the proper care and attention the plants can rebound in 12 months, she said.

◆ Become a volunteer. Many botanical community organizations need volunteers. Williams recommends joining local garden clean-up crews, beautification projects or community plant societies. In addition to providing a community service, you'll meet other gardeners, including those who are a source of knowledge and or plant clippings. Many times community gardens will have plant sales with great prices.

◆ Harvest your own. Williams recommends saving the seeds from your own garden. With those seeds you can grow small plants indoors before replanting the seedlings in an outdoor garden. This strategy will provide you with a supply to trade or give to other gardeners. Williams also recommends perennial plants, which should be divided every three to five years. FD

The Yellow Room

Nearly every room in my Dream House overlooks the garden. The Yellow Room, however, offers the best view of the Royal Palm trees, the pool, and bright-leafed bougainvilleas. Tucked near the northern staircase, the Yellow Room provides a corner of privacy in that open house. It's an ideal room for a library, an office, or a guest room.

When I was a child during the 1960s, we didn't have an official guest room in our suburban home, but we always had room for visitors, including my grandmother Julia.

To make room for guests, my parents moved the kids into one room or set up guest quarters in the bedroom on the lower floor of our split-level home. That room had its own "powder room." Fresh linens, towels, and pretty soaps were added to make our guest feel comfortable in our home.

A guest room for less

Creating a comfortable but affordable room for guests can be a challenge. But it's possible to make your home more inviting without spending a lot of money.

Furnish a multi-tasking room. Tammy, a Miami Beach homeowner, designates her guest room for many chores. On weekday mornings, the guest room—a spare bedroom with its own bathroom—doubles as a home office. In the evenings, the spare room becomes a media center for her children. But on weekends, when guests typically arrive, the furniture makes for a bed and breakfast atmosphere. For instance, a large cabinet—the family media center—doubles as a guest closet, complete with clothing hooks and a stock of extra pillows and linens. Likewise, a couch easily converts into a comfortable bed—with a festive quilt—for weekend guests.

Create a gift basket. From sunscreen to new toothbrushes, Tammy provides guests with a large stock of personal care products in an attractive basket. She purchases travel-size containers of shampoo, lotions, and other grooming products, which are refilled from economy-sized bottles as needed.

Establish a privacy zone. The ideal guest room or suite enables a guest to retreat behind a closed door, complete with a private bathroom. (If you don't have an extra bathroom for guests, *Woman's World* magazine recommends placing an attractive towel stand in the guest room.) The guest area should also include ample space for suitcases, clothing, and other personal belongings.

Use color wisely. Walls painted in soothing colors, such as soft greens and aqua blues, can create a relaxing retreat for guests, said Jane Heaton, owner of Designing Woman, a design firm. She recommends avoiding wild and hot colors, which can make some guests feel claustrophobic in an enclosed area.

Decorate with a theme. Use accents and accessories to create a vacation environment, Heaton said. She recommends tropical, nautical or fishing themes. Mounted seashells, unusual picture frames, photographs, and other accessories can provide decorative accents. Potpourri, scented soap, and other aromatic treats also create a relaxing environment.

Stock up. Supplies of festive hand paper towels, fluffy cotton towels, appliances (reading lights, an iron, and a clock), and extra pillows will make guests feel pampered. In my home, we also provide visitors with a wide selection of reading materials: novels, non-fiction books, and magazines.

Be prepared for extra sleepers. An inflatable air mattress, additional blankets, sleeping bags, and cots are also helpful if guests arrive with children.

Grandmother Julia Comes to Visit

When my grandmother came to visit us, she often traveled from Philadelphia to South Jersey using public transportation, her favorite mode of traveling. My grandmother was in her late 40s when she finally learned to drive a car. Likewise, I don't drive either. I have an irrational fear of cars. Just like my grandmother, I get around by walking, carpooling, or taking public transportation.

When I was 12 years old my grandmother came to visit, but it was a different kind of visit. She had been in the hospital and after she was released, she came to our house to recuperate.

The day grandmother arrived, junior high school let out at 3:00 p.m. as usual, and I was home by 3:20. I opened the side door of our split-level home and ran into the family room with a loud, "Hello Grandma." She smiled, but there was not enough room on her face to contain her smile. Numbness crept through me like a thief, robbing me of good manners. I just stared at her. My face felt stiff and hard like the stale bubble gum sticks packed with the trading cards.

"Hello," she said. Her eyes were hungry, like a new kid in school who really wanted a friend.

Julia made room for me on the sofa, moving as if she were lifting a great weight. But she was thinner than I was, and I was a skinny little kid. Watching her move, I felt lost in an awful fairy tale. I was Red Riding Hood and the wolf had eaten my grandmother.

But once I sat down, I felt warmer. The family room looked the same. The couch was the same knobby fabric that made my legs itch. And

Julia was still my grandmother, the same woman who punctuated almost every conversation with, "And yes, G-d is good."

So I kissed her cheekbone and we began watching an *Addams Family* re-run. Or at least I watched the show. Julia watched me. I could feel her eyes on my face, hungry for my smiles and laughter. She smiled when I smiled, laughed when I laughed. It must have been a very funny show because I laughed hard and loud.

My brother Ben and younger sisters Karen and Debbie came home from elementary school some time around 4:00. Usually after school, we played kickball or tag in the street with the other neighborhood kids. But no matter how many times that doorbell rang for us, no one went out to play that afternoon. We stayed in the family room with Julia, watching re-run after re-run: *Gilligan's Island, Batman,* and *The Flintstones.* We just wanted to sit there, smiling at the TV.

We didn't have a guest room, but no one complained about sharing a room or sleeping near the laundry room, and no one talked about how sick Grandma looked. We just watched her shuffle in her bathrobe and slippers from the family room to the kitchen to the bedroom, hugging herself tighter with each step as if she were scared of slipping away.

She stayed with us for just over a week. One day I came home from school and she was gone. Mom explained that Julia had to go back to the hospital for more treatment and then she would stay at my great Uncle John's house. About a week after Julia left our house, the phone rang at 7 a.m. as we were getting up for school. Immediately, I knew. No one ever called that early with good news.

I rinsed my face in the bathroom and walked to the kitchen where my mother was crying.

Beyond the sadness and tears, my grandmother's passing touched us in so many ways. In fact, those last days with my grandmother Julia provided a lasting lesson in the importance of opening our hearts and homes to friends and relatives, in sickness and in health. I learned that it doesn't have to cost a lot to make someone feel comfortable in our home. Fluffy towels and fancy guest suites are nice, but not really necessary when we try to create priceless moments for guests. FD

Getting Away From It All

My grandmother's funeral haunts me with images of crumpled tissues, salty tears, and paper fans on sticks. During the service, the church sisters (dignified volunteers in white uniforms and lace) waved their paper fans and smelling salts at our tears.

Finding me in a front pew, the church sisters—like angels or nurses—held me while a parade of black hats and suits paused in front of my grandmother's open casket. Some people touched Julia's hand or her hair. Others called her name. After that service, it was a long while before my family went back to church.

Instead some Sunday mornings during the mid-1970s we'd get up early and drive to Atlantic City where we rode bicycles on the boardwalk, which has been around since 1870. I loved Atlantic City, the old Atlantic City, before glitzy gambling casinos replaced familiar landmarks. I still remember the Steel Pier amusement park and the old delis that sold foot-long hot dogs covered in mustard, relish, and sauerkraut. Walking on the boardwalk, travelers were greeted by the aroma of freshly-roasted peanuts and the sugared glaze of saltwater taffies that stuck to our teeth. I even loved the old musty hotels that smelled like my great-grandmother's attic.

On bikes, we pedaled past souvenir shops that sold shell necklaces and tie-dyed T-shirts. Tired and hungry, sometimes we stopped for breakfast at small coffee shops that served all-you-can-eat breakfast buffets of scrambled eggs, link sausages, pancakes, and buttery grits. And some Easter Sundays—dressed in our casual clothes—we'd watch the famous Atlantic City Easter Bonnet parade.

I liked the pretty hats, and I remembered the pastel bonnets, buttoned-wrist gloves and the white patent leather shoes that I used to wear to my grandmother's church. But at the Jersey shore on the edge of the Atlantic Ocean, I gladly traded my church shoes for the early morning wind on my face. I loved the smell of the salt air and the ocean crashing into the sand. That was G-d to me and I knew that my grandmother would approve. She always said G-d was everywhere—even in Atlantic City.

Family vacations were sacred in our house and those get-aways were a consecrated block of time in which my parents could let go of work-related worries and anxieties in order to focus only on family and fun.

With my father driving, we took long road trips during the 1960s and 1970s. Back then plane travel was considered a rare luxury, but even now—when flights are affordable—auto trips are a frugal option for family travel. In fact, trips by car, camper or RV and trucks represent nearly 80 percent of domestic trips.

"A family can save hundreds of dollars otherwise spent on airline tickets and destination rental cars by driving," according to the Consumer Credit Counseling Service.

Our road trip vacation destinations varied. One year, we rented a cabin on Lake Erie and another summer, we drove to Gainesville, Florida, where my mother attended a conference on Early Childhood Education at the University of Florida. We saved money by staying in the small apartment that was assigned to my mother for the conference.

Canada was also a favorite spot on our vacation map. We often drove to Niagara Falls, where we wore black rubber rain coats while standing on a ledge behind the famous falls.

During our visits to Niagara Falls, we always stayed at the Sheraton Poste Inn, our favorite hotel in Canada. We loved the Train Room, a ground floor guest suite with windows that faced railroad tracks and provided a close (and audible) view of rumbling trains. My siblings and I were amazed that our Train Room was always empty and available to us whenever we arrived.

Looking back, I recognize the Train Room as the ultimate two-for-one special: My parents were able to book affordable rooms in a ground floor suite that other guests avoided, and we—my brother, sisters and I—enjoyed the free entertainment and excitement of thundering trains on the other side of our hotel window. It was all a matter of perspective. Vacations, I discovered, provide a playground for learning.

"Showing children you can have fun without spending hundreds of dollars is an important lesson in their financial literacy education," said Jessica Cecere, president of Consumer Credit Counseling Service of Palm Beach.

Savvy travel tips

Decades later I still love trains and I enjoy traveling on Amtrak. And now that my parents and my sister Karen all live in Central Florida, I often travel from Miami to Orlando by train. I have picked up several money-saving tips while traveling.

1. Compare prices. On one outing, my round-trip fare from Miami to Orlando was cheaper than Greyhound and more comfortable than a bus ride. The round-trip fare was also cheaper than auto travel, if I consider gas, tolls, and the wear-and-tear on our temperamental minivan.

2. Discounts at AAA. I could have saved more by using our AAA (American Automobile Association) membership discount. But discounts only apply if a trip is booked at least three days in advance.

3. Don't overpack. Once, I traveled with several gifts

stuffed into a large suitcase. Bad move. The porter told me that my suitcase was 20 pounds overweight. I had to pay $2 extra for a box and in the station, I had to repack and repackage my bundles. What a pain. I wasted time and money.

4. Budget your time for delays. The train left on time but arrived two hours late.

5. Pack earphones, a DVD player or a laptop PC. My seatmate had a portable DVD player, with a great selection of films, including the 2005 version of *Pride and Prejudice*. I watched in silence (with her approval), and I could have plugged in to listen if I had brought along my own earphones. DVD players are popular items and Amtrak has outlets near each set of seats.

6. Don't drink the coffee. I wasted $1.75 on a cup of horrible coffee. The server was kind but the coffee was a waste of cream and sugar. (Amtrak should outsource its coffee bar to Starbucks.)

7. Bring work. I worked on a book review and assorted other projects while traveling on the train.

8. Relax and look out the window. There are financial and spiritual benefits to meditation.

9. Bring your own snacks. It's allowed!

10. Discounts and promotions. Check online for discounts and promotions at *www.amtrak.com.* There are other discounts for seniors, students, and frequent travelers. It pays to ask. And when traveling with kids, ask for special rates and giveaways at the ticket counter. On past trips, my kids have received a few cute gifts from Amtrak.

Disney World for Less

Orlando is also home to Disney World. Given the relatively short distance between Miami and Orlando, my husband and I frequently take our kids to the Magic Kingdom, Universal Studios, and other theme parks in that corner of Central Florida.

The American Automobile Association (AAA) offers its members a variety of discounts for Disney parks, Universal Studios, Sea World and other theme parks in different parts of the country. Check your area or the area where you plan to visit for deals.

Free drinks at Epcot

I discovered a great way to get free sodas at Epcot, the international and futuristic park at Disney World in Orlando.

In early 2007, my family had all the free soda we wanted to drink at Epcot. (Water is our beverage of choice. But soda is a nice treat.) Follow these steps to save a bundle:

1. Go to the Cool Club exhibit in the Future World section of Epcot. It's a small display and showroom run by Coca-Cola. (Ask a park employee for directions.)

2. Find the soda fountain exhibit.

3. Get a paper cup (free) and taste the bottomless samples of Coca-Cola sodas from all over the world. Our favorites were China (a watermelon taste), Israel (a lemony-sprite flavor), and Germany (tasted like spicy ginger ale).

4. Skip the Italian soda button if you don't like bitter-tasting tonic. This was our prank flavor that we offered to unsuspecting members of our group.

5. Go back often during the course of your visit to Epcot.

6. Also drink the free water from the (very clean) Disney fountains.

Theme park tips

1. Bring your own rain coats or ponchos. Of course, when it rains, theme park gift shops have ample supplies of rain gear for about $6 per poncho. That's convenient, but for a family of four, that's $24, plus tax, that could be saved or spent on other vacation treats. In contrast, you can buy ponchos for a buck a piece at Walgreens and dollar store chains.

2. Pack sweatshirts or extra clothing. When the sun goes down, especially in the winter and spring, temperatures sometimes dip sharply in the parks. We've been in Orlando during the December Holiday season when the thermometer has dipped into the low 30s. Brrr. I've watched in sympathy as tourists in shorts, halter tops, and bathing suits have purchased warmer clothing at gifts shops, with prices that start at $25 for a sweatshirt. (Been there, done that.) We bring our own jackets and check the forecast before leaving our home or hotel room. Extra clothes can be stored in a park locker.

3. Carry your own snacks. As special treats, we occasionally buy the park-branded snacks (ice cream, soda, or candy). But most of our snacks are from the DIY (Do-It-Yourself) label. Likewise, bring your own water bottles. It's best to freeze the bottles the night before (in your hotel room) and sip the defrosting water in the hot park.

4. Enjoy spray-and-soak rides in the middle of the day, when you'll dry off faster in the hot sun. Otherwise, you'll be tempted to buy new gear at one of the conveniently located clothing stores in the park.

5. Get a room with perks. A great hotel—with lots of free activities and services—will save you hundreds of dollars during a vacation. That's because the more your hotel offers, the fewer days your children will want to spend in the park, which translates into fewer admission tickets, meals, and treats. For instance, with my extended family, we have frequently stayed at a kid-centric resort in the Orlando area that offered free entertainment, crafts, games, miniature golf, and sporting events for families.

What's more, the main pool—with water sprays, fountains, and other fun surprises—was like a water park. Once, we even had to bribe our kids to get out of the pool in order to use the theme park tickets that we had already spent a fortune on. We didn't make that mistake twice.

6. Check out free or low-cost attractions. Orlando has more to offer than Disney or Universal Studios. There are many frugal entertainment options that cost a fraction of theme park admission tickets. This logic applies to other areas of the country.

Lesser known—and cheaper—local attractions often try to ride the coattails of nationally known parks. There are also municipal parks, zoos, museums, and other affordable attractions.

7. Shop outside the park. Many of the dollar stores and gift shops on the nearby highways carry affordable souvenirs and trinkets.

8. Give each child a trip budget. We provide our children with a trip allowance to spend as they choose. Of course, we cover the basics, but for "buy-me, buy-me" trinkets, the kids are on their own and when their fun money runs out, that's it.

9. Don't overstay. Kids nine and under have about a six-hour window in the park. My husband and I have timed our kids, and we have watched the temper tantrum cycles of other children. Trust me. Don't stay in the park with irritable, tired, and grumpy children. You will feel as if you have wasted a ton of money.

Instead, leave the park and get your hands marked with a re-entry stamp. Go back to your hotel for naps and consider returning to the park for evening parades, fireworks, or other festivities. Mothers with younger children can also go to the nursing station in some Disney parks. This facility—with rocking chairs, microwave ovens, televisions, and play areas—is an ideal "chill zone" when you and your toddler or baby need a time-out.

10. Find the playgrounds. Inside amusement parks and municipal parks are real playgrounds where the kids can just play and get exercise. A constant diet of theme parks represents too much passive entertainment. Sometimes, kids and adults just need to play and run around.

11. Opt for free Internet at the library. Don't be a snob when traveling. Internet cafes may have great coffee, but public libraries have a wide assortment of computer terminals, programs, and Internet service—all free of charge. Indeed, I've spent hours at the public library in Kissimmee, Florida, while vacationing with my family in Orlando.

At that library, my kids enjoyed a literary break from the overwhelming amusement park scene, and I was able to log on to the Internet free of charge. It was a win-win for everyone, and my boys enjoyed using the computer terminals in the extensive children's section.

Luxury for Less

I love Disney, but for less than the cost of an amusement park vacation, including a one-day visit to the park, we paid for luxury accommodations, meals, entertainment, and transportation. We treated ourselves to a luxurious, but frugal vacation in our own neighborhood.

Here's how we did it:

1. Luxury Resort. We looked for a high-end resort, with off-season prices. We also searched for other discounts, including Florida resident rates and AAA membership discounts. The off-season rate at the Grove Isle Hotel & Spa is $199, with the local resident discount rate of $149. That's a lot less than the peak season nightly rate of at least $529, excluding tax, tips, and parking.

2. Creative Meals. Our family of five spent less than $85 on a total of four meals during our vacation. The room was equipped with a refrigerator, and we brought our own food and a sandwich press (a mini grill).

The room also came with complimentary coffee, and we brought our own cake. For special treats, we purchased café lattes, smoothies, and other goodies from Starbucks and other small shops. Our big-ticket meal expense: We spent $53, plus tip, at a very nice restaurant. It was an elegant way to end our trip.

3. Avoid the mini-bar in the room. Faced with lofty price tags of $60 a bottle, we avoided the mini-bar in our room. Very pricey stuff, with fine labels. I even managed to avoid the little boxes of G-diva chocolate, which were richly priced. Very tempting. (We purchased a large bar of high-end chocolate later at regular retail prices. It was worth the wait.)

We did, however, break down and open three cans of sodas from the bar stock. (We forgot to pack beverages.) But to avoid the high charges, we replaced the sodas with low-priced (exact) duplicates from a nearby convenience store.

Other Quick Tips

♦ Stay local to avoid road trip costs.

♦ Explore quaint, old historical neighborhoods that you rarely visit.

♦ Find a local resort that feels far from home.

♦ Stay at a resort that has complimentary Internet and a free business center. (At other resorts, I've paid hefty fees to log-on and use the computers, fax machines and other office equipment.)

♦ Select a resort with a free fitness center. Some places charge extra for use of the spa and gym. (High-end spa treatments are typically extra.)

♦ Get tips about local points of interest from residents or experts. Stay near an area with a vibrant night life. Once we left our resort area, there was a lot to do in a neighboring shopping district.

Our trip represented our attempt to experiment with off-season rates in a tropical resort near our home town. Altogether we paid $205 for a snippet of paradise. We had a view of the water, a full balcony, free unlimited use of a computer with Internet access, beautiful walking trails, a free refrigerator in the room, and a free morning newspaper (delivered in an elegant leather pouch).

"The cost of a hotel room can be one of the biggest expenses during travel. If you want a wallet-friendly vacation, go off-season," said Marita Hudson, a spokeswoman for *www.CheapTickets.com*, an online service. CheapTickets also publishes a quarterly "Off-Season Deals Report," which is a market-by-market rundown of off-peak prices in various cities.

Below is a chart of Discount Travel Websites. And don't forget to check out hotel and resort websites for their Internet-only specials, too. FD

Discount Travel Websites		
Site	**Details**	**Special**
www.Priceline.com	Flights, hotels, cars, packages, cruises, tours, and attractions	Price Breakers (last-minute flights throughout U.S.)
www.Hotels.com	Flights, condos/B&B, and vacation packages	Red Hot Deals
www.SkyAuction.com	Flights, cruises, and vacation rentals	Hot Travel Deals
www.Travelocity.com	Vacation packages, flights, hotels, cars /rail, cruises, and activities	Last Minute Packages
www.Expedia.com	Flights, hotels, cars, vacation packages, cruises, activities, and business travel	Deals and Destinations
www.Orbitz.com	Hotels, vacation packages, cruises, and activities	Deals

Bleach: The Fragrance of Love

Whether leaving for a few hours or a few weeks, my parents had certain pre-trip rituals designed to protect our home and our homecoming. For example, before a short trip, every lock on every entrance—the side door, the front door, the garage door—was inspected and bolted against would-be intruders. And a thick wooden pole was wedged into the track of the sliding glass door that led to the backyard porch, thereby barring the rear entrance of our home.

Lights were left on in the kitchen, living room, and hallway. Those security lights cast shadows like ghosts, guarding our home while we were away. And finally, the porch light was always on, brightening the path up the long cement stairs and making it easier for us to find our way to the front door.

Longer trips were more complicated. Arrangements had to be made for newspapers, mail, and the large square gallon milk dispenser that was delivered to our home on a weekly basis. Neighbors and friends were notified and on-call to check our home and to water the lawn. All windows were secured, appliances stored away, and the air conditioning set at a level to help combat mold and odors during the humid months.

And finally, we had to clean and clean and clean. As a child, I never understood this cleaning ritual, but my parents were insistent. The house had to welcome us back, and we had to have a clean house to come home to. That was the rule M&D laid out for us as they passed out mops, rags, and brooms. We groaned, but complied. We knew better than to argue; their faces had that look that ended all discussions.

In a worn blue bucket with a metal handle that was partially covered by rubber, my mother mixed chemicals as if she were making one of her special homemade soups. Into the boiling hot water, she poured Pine Sol, a clear amber liquid that smelled like the tall pine trees at the foot of our backyard hill. Or she added Mr. Clean, a yellow liquid with a medicinal smell. And with her hands protected by yellow rubber gloves, Mom wrung out rags, sponges, and mops that were wiped over almost every horizontal surface in our home.

In the bathrooms, Ajax—a white powder that turned blue when wet—was sprinkled on the bathtub, the toilet and the ceramic tiles. And sometimes, when they were having a real clean fit, M&D used discarded toothbrushes to clean the spaces between the small pink and blue speckled tiles on the bathroom floor. And after everything was cleaned, rinsed, and polished, a coat of Clorox bleach—heavily diluted—sanitized our home. Bleach was the smell of love in my parents' home.

Plain old vinegar

My mom has also believed in the cleaning power of non-toxic cleaners such as baking soda and vinegar. Her faith was well-placed. Plain old vinegar and elbow grease are valuable products for beating back mildew, grease, and other household problems. That's the word from a blog reader named George Knox, who is poetical about the virtues of vinegar.

"Check out vinegar as a miracle fluid," George wrote in an email. "[Vinegar] kills weeds and makes flowers grow, removes rust, cleans stains and kills fleas. There are a number of websites dealing with its value—and it is among the cheapest items in the supermarket."

The product is among the many simple solutions touted by *Consumer Reports* in the classic text *How to Clean Practically Anything*, which is available at bookstores and through various online vendors. White vinegar, according to the editorial team at *Consumer Reports*, "is good for a variety of household cleaning tasks, including removing carpet stains, clearing clogged drains, and cleaning coffeemakers, chrome, cookware and countertops."

The vinegar fan club also includes Amy Allen Clark, founder of *www.MomAdvice.com* and representative for a national cleaning products company. Here are vinegar two tips she shared with me:

Use vinegar as a rinse. There's no need to buy fancy products for the rinse cycle of your dishwasher, because vinegar works just as well, Clark said. For newer models, pour a quarter cup of vinegar into the rinse dispenser. For models without a rinse dispenser, add a quarter cup of vinegar to the door dispenser during the first rinse cycle, which should be indicated by a dial or panel on the outside of your machine. During the rinse cycle, the vinegar will circulate and remove residue. "Vinegar is great for removing spots on dishes," Clark said.

Vinegar can clean your dishwasher. Place a bowl with two cups of vinegar upright on the lower rack. Then run the empty dishwasher without detergent to thoroughly clean the interior.

Clark went on to share with me other practical kitchen clean-up tips.

Step-savers during cooking. "Make sure your dishwasher is empty when you prepare a meal," Clark said. An empty dishwasher encourages a clean-as-you-go mentality, saving time in the long run. As you cook, lightly rinse off utensils. You'll have less to clean after dinner and less heavy-duty scrubbing.

Soak dishes during meals. Fill a sink or plastic tub with cold water and dishwashing detergent. During cooking and dining, soak sticky or especially dirty pans or dishes. This process reduces scrubbing when they're washed in hot water later.

Use cooking sprays. A spritz of nonstick cooking spray in pans before cooking makes dishwashing easier. Cooking sprays also help prevent food stains in plastic containers.

Baking soda 101

Arm & Hammer, the maker of a popular baking soda, has a long list of affordable cleanup tips for kitchens, yards, and other areas of the home. The tips are well organized on their company website, *www.armhammer.com*, providing an online, room-by-room baking soda tour of your home with recipes and unusual uses for the product. The name brand version of this versatile product is cheap, but generic baking soda also works well and costs even less.

Here's an example of the information I found on the Arm & Hammer website:

Deodorize the waste bin. "Lightly sprinkle baking soda. Apply regularly as you add to the container or when empty. Wash the container with a solution of 1 cup of baking soda per 1 gallon of water."

Scrub a tub. "Sprinkle baking soda lightly on a clean damp sponge and scrub as usual. Rinse thoroughly and wipe dry. Afterwards, take a nice relaxing bath without the worry of harsh chemicals."

"There are so many reasons, including these, why there is always baking soda in my house," said fellow blogger Kyleen at *www.Texan Newyorker.wordpress.com*. "It's also good for removing sticky adhesive residue from plastic and glass, and for removing cooked-on food particles from pots and pans (salt works, too, if they're REALLY dirty).

The WD-40 fan club

Of all the cleaning products in the world, WD-40 is the wonder product in my Miami Beach apartment. For example, when our sliding glass door gets stuck, my husband sprays the track with WD-40, a great lubricant. But there are so many more uses, including cleaning piano keys, removing crayon from walls, lifting off baked-on cookie batter from baking tins, and un-sticking old tape.

The WD-40 Company's website, *www.wd40.com*, lists 2,000 uses of

WD-40, a multipurpose spray that lubricates and "displaces" water, according to Liza Gaoiran, WD-40's brand manager.

"It actually came out of a campaign where we solicited uses for WD-40 from consumers. They figured out more uses than we could," Gaoiran said.

♦ Use to loosen rusty nuts and screws.

♦ Clean garden tools.

♦ Clean piano keys.

♦ Keep wicker chairs from squeaking.

♦ Lubricate small rolling toys.

♦ Keep garden tools rust-free.

♦ Clean patio door glide strip.

♦ Remove crayon from clothes dryer
  (make sure to unplug dryer first).

♦ Remove scuff marks from ceramic tile floor.

♦ Keep metal wind chimes rust-free.

♦ Remove crayon from walls.

Your wood furniture

Taking good care of wood furniture can get very expensive. But there are also frugal solutions for tables and woodwork. Most of the expensive products on the market lack the punch of simpler tools—such as a bit of paste wax and a cloth moistened with soap and warm water—according to an article written by Teri Masaschi, who owns a furniture and restoration business in New Mexico.

Here's the rundown on furniture polishes, sprays, and oils:

♦ Aerosol sprays and liquids. Sprays and oils (silicone-based, emulsion blends or oil polishes) are the easiest to apply and the most popular. But if this is your favorite furniture tool, use it for cleaning, not shining. And within this category, emulsion polishes—milky blends of oil and water—are most effective at removing grease and dust, but leave minimal shine. "A cloth dampened in warm, soapy water cleans just as well," Masaschi said.

♦ Beware of furniture oils. For the short run, petroleum or mineral-based products leave your furniture with a slick gleam. In fact, quick-sale antique dealers love this short-lived shine. But over the long-term, the oil that remains on the surface really attracts dirt and dust. "So it's better to avoid this type of polish," Masaschi said.

♦ High marks for paste wax. *Fine Woodworking* magazine recommends the regular use of a dab of paste wax as protective maintenance for furniture. A thin application of paste wax provides a longer shine—relative to oils and sprays—and conceals minor blemishes on the surface. Masaschi recommends Briwax, Staples, Antiquax, and Liberon's Black Bison. Caution: while great for protecting and polishing, paste wax is not suitable for cleaning furniture.

♦ Microfiber cloth and water. *Fine Woodworking* recommends old-school, low-tech methods for maintaining furniture in between wax applications. Dust off furniture with a microfiber cloth, a nonabrasive material made from polyester and polyamide, with a strand count of 200,000 strands per square inch. Microfiber cloths can be purchased at drugstores, office supply and auto supply stores, and cost from $3.50 to $8. The cloths can be washed and re-used. Remove grime with a cloth dampened with soap and water.

Jenn, a blogger with Frugal Upstate, (*www.frugalupstate.blogspot.com*) shares her big find on microfiber cloths:

"Dollar Tree stores near me carry microfiber cloths for, of course, a dollar. I can't tell the difference between them and the more expensive ones," she said.

My ABCs of laundry

Every floor in our building has a washer and dryer, which are operated by using plastic debit cards. With each load costing $3, I know that I would save money on laundry if we were to move into my Dream House.

But I don't fantasize about washing clothes in the Mediterranean. I have a lot of dreams about that house, but doing laundry isn't one of them.

In fact, during all my tours of the Mediterranean, I've never visited The Laundry Room. And I don't care what kind of energy-efficient, step-saving, new-age appliances are plugged into the wall sockets of my Dream House. I have no desire to see that room.

Since my teen years, The Laundry Room has been my household nemesis. In high school, for example, I was assigned hamper duty, which consisted of washing, drying, and folding the family laundry. But instead of managing that chore, I often sat in the laundry room with a novel. Not surprisingly, Home Economics was not my best class.

Now that I'm a parent, I have a new spin on laundry dramas. Consider the math: Multiply three children by seven towels a week. Add 15 sets of school uniforms and several I-wore-it-for-a-minute shirts. With that mix, laundry becomes a major investment in terms of time and money.

Determined to finally score an "A" in Home Economics, I've done my homework. I've accumulated the following tips from my parents, detergent companies, appliance experts, and other personal care sources:

Organization. Like many things in life, good organization is the key. The makers of Tide, for example, recommend a well-stocked, well-organized laundry room that is convenient to the rest of your home. Reduce sorting time by setting up different hampers for different colors (color, white, and dark clothes) and fabric types. In my home, I've tried to eliminate the double-digit towel cycle, by assigning each member of the family two towels for the week. That should reduce weekly towel usage to 10 towels from a current high of about 30.

Drying. And speaking of towels, you can speed up the drying time of any load by adding a large dry towel to a damp load. This step could cut your drying time (and costs) by 25 percent or more, according to The Laundry Alternative, a Vermont-based appliance company, which specializes in eco-friendly laundry and septic system products.

Detergent. We can all save money by carefully measuring detergent. Many consumers waste money and resources by using more laundry detergent than necessary, according to The Laundry Alternative. If you live in an area with soft water, use less detergent to wash laundry.

Corey K. Tournet, owner of The Laundry Alternative, said in an email that the term "hard water" was coined because it is "harder" to wash clothes in it than "soft water."

Battle of the wrinkles

Believe it or not, I actually enjoy ironing. It's a form of meditation that I picked up from my dad, who also loves to iron. But if you hate ironing, the manufacturers of Tide detergent have a few suggestions.

♦ Wash lightly soiled and bright color items in cold water to reduce wrinkles. (A cold water wash also saves energy and money.)

♦ Shake out your clothes before transferring them to the dryer. This step prevents clothes from becoming wrinkled or balled up.

♦ Don't overstuff the dryer; clothes do not properly circulate in an overstuffed dryer.

♦ Fold or hang up garments immediately after the dryer stops spinning or else you'll have a tangled heap of wrinkled items. FD

Back to School on a Tight Budget

No amount of pre-vacation cleaning would have made it easier for us to return home from our Caribbean vacation in August of 1972. The late summer air already tasted like fall, and Philadelphia felt so cold.

Even the newspaper headlines—visible and bold as we walked through the airport—gave us the chills: SCHOOL STRIKE! The Philadelphia Teachers Union had declared a strike, and my parents, school teachers, were out of jobs during the work stoppage.

Initially, my parents did not cross the picket line. They were loyal union members, but as the strike wore on for weeks and weeks, M&D made hard choices. My mother found an administrative position at the

Camden County School District, where she was hired to help manage the public school day care centers.

And after several sleepless nights, my father crossed the picket line. The Teachers Union had been good to him; he was a loyal union man. But he had a family to feed and children to teach.

The jeers and anger of union members in front of his school haunted him as he walked past the strikers and into the classroom. What's more, some of his fellow teachers stopped speaking to him socially, and long after the strike was ended they refused to work with my father on school projects.

For me the strike felt real when I went shopping for back-to-school supplies. The fancy spiral notebooks with shiny covers, the ten-pack of cute erasers in rainbow shades and the wacky pens were not on my list. I purchased only what I really needed for my freshman year at Cherry Hill High School West. Nor did I shop for back-to-school clothes. On the first day of school, I wore the same two-piece navy blue matching skirt and top outfit that my mother and I had picked out for our vacation. It was almost new. I learned a lot about money that fall, and I was carefully tutored on the difference between wants and needs.

Back-to-school shopping

As a learning tool, back-to-school shopping is a great opportunity to teach kids fundamental lessons about money. I bring along my kids on supply-shopping trips, and I'm not alone.

Nationwide, about 53 percent of families use back-to-school shopping to deliver lessons about money management, according to a recent survey.

That makes sense, given the amount of money we spend during the annual back-to-school shopping spree. In the fall of 2007, the typical family spent about $563.49 in back-to-school shopping and as a nation, we spent over $18 billion on clothes, school supplies, and gadgets for the new school year, according to the National Retail Federation.

We live close to several stores, including Walgreens, CVS, Office Depot, and Target. Using newspaper flyers and online price checks, we compare advertised prices and stock up on supplies that we will need

Fall 2007 Back-to-School Shopping Lists	
Item	People who considered it their highest expense
Clothing	64%
Books	13%
Supplies	9%

throughout the school year. Meanwhile, our PTA offers cheap, tax-free prices at their supply store. eBay is also a great spot for finding bargains in school supplies. Here are my other back-to-school shopping tips:

Shop at home. Every year I over-shop for supplies—I know this because at the end of the school year my children bring home supplies that have been barely touched. As a result, I've begun to examine our existing supplies before shopping for new stuff. This inventory process has saved us a bundle in time and money.

Look for sales tax holidays. Across the country, various states provide a tax-free shopping window for school supplies. In Florida, for example, we have about a week in late July or early August. Other states that have offered back-to-school tax holidays include: Alabama, Connecticut, District of Columbia, Georgia, Iowa, Maryland, Missouri, New Mexico, North Carolina, South Carolina, Tennessee, Texas, and Virginia.

Purchase floor models. The floor sample—especially if it has a few nicks and dents—may come packaged with a steep discount. This applies to clothing, backpacks, calculators, and computers. My husband and I, for example, paid $168 for a $350 digital camera that was marked down because it was a floor model.

"Today's students often need more sophisticated supplies than their parents needed," said Jessica Cecere, a regional president of Consumer Credit Counseling Services (CCCS). "The demands of their academic programs may require personal computers, calculators, and expensive lab fees. Without careful planning, families may be forced to choose between their child's educational needs and household bills. Back-to-school sales, thrift stores, and recycling last year's clothing and supplies are all supplements to the most important step a family can take: budgeting."

Yard sales and secondhand stores. From school uniforms to supplies, many secondhand outlets have back-to-school merchandise in either excellent or even new condition. While visiting Pittsburgh for my sister's wedding, we popped into a secondhand store in an upscale neighborhood and found a blue uniform dress, new with tags, for less than $5.

Hand-me downs. Public and private schools, community groups, and even friends are valuable sources of hand-me-down clothes and uniforms. Some schools, for example, maintain a bank of donated school uniforms that are in excellent condition. Keep in mind that children typically outgrow clothes before wearing them out.

"Clothing swaps and hand-me-downs are a great way not only to save money, but to extend the life of resources that have already been manufactured," according to a statement from the Center for a New American Dream.

Lifetime warranties. JanSport and other companies sell backpacks with lifetime warranties. "Even if an old backpack no longer zips correctly or has rips or tears, you can often send it back to the company for repair or replacement—at absolutely no charge," according to the Center for New American Dream.

Lifetime warrantees are a frugal option, said Sally, a blogger with Through a Glass Darkly. "I think backpacks are one area where it makes sense to pay a good chunk now to get something of quality. And sometimes you can find JanSport bags at discount stores like TJ Maxx," Sally said. "I convinced my mother to buy me a JanSport in 8th grade—it was $50, so this convincing took a lot of work—and 13 years later, it's still going strong. My husband has had a similar experience with his LL Bean backpack."

Recycled Paper and Binders. For rough drafts, notes, and household projects, we save money with our DIY recycled paper—the flip side of used paper. And when printing out notes or files from the computer, I often use both sides of the paper. Likewise, we try to get additional mileage from binders that are used but are in excellent condition.

My oldest son—a high school student—recently discovered the benefits of recycling. In his travels, he came across a group of students who were cleaning out lockers and backpacks as the school year concluded. To my son's amazement, some of the students emptied unused school supplies into a trash bin, including new or barely used notebooks. My son retrieved a few of the pristine notebooks and got a head start on our annual back-to-school preparations. ꟻＤ

I Got Accepted, Now What?

With school teachers for parents, my siblings and I were well-schooled on the importance of education. In addition to getting good grades, we were expected to attend college, and my parents made many financial sacrifices to put us through school. For instance, my folks did not drive late model cars, nor did they install a built-in pool in our backyard. But they always found money for music lessons, family vacations, and college tuition bills.

The value of a college education can be measured in hard cash. The U.S. Department of Labor estimates that—on average—an employee with a college degree earns about $1 million more than a worker with only a high school diploma over the course of a lifetime. For my parents—the first college graduates in each of their immediate families—a college education was a badge of honor and family pride. Therefore, when I was accepted at Georgetown University in the spring of 1976, my parents were elated, even though my annual college bills translated into the price of a new car each year for four years. And that was just for the basic expenses, before books, clothing, and other costs of dorm life. Since then, college costs have grown faster than inflation over the last few decades.

"The discouraging reality is that college costs have skyrocketed and federal financial aid has eroded," said Dallas Martin, President of the National Association of Student Financial Aid Administrators (NASFAA). "The result is that the doors of educational opportunity have closed for many of our nation's youth because they cannot afford to attend college."

To finance four college tuition bills—including the cost of three kids on campus at the same time—my parents saved a portion of each paycheck, took out a second loan on their home and made other financial arrangements. For instance, to make Georgetown more affordable, my parents also enrolled in a third-party tuition program. For a fee, the service paid my yearly tuition bills and collected monthly payments, plus financing, from my parents. Additionally, we applied for financial aid from Georgetown University, and I received a small work-study grant of $800 annually, which covered a portion of my day-to-day living expenses while I was at school.

On-the-job education

Work-study programs bridge the fiscal gap between professional aspirations and the five-figure annual costs of higher education. Most colleges and universities offer a diverse mix of work-study programs, which provide student workers with a paycheck, work experience, and flexible schedules. The various programs involve federal, state, and private funds.

Under the Federal Work Study program, the U.S. government provides colleges and universities with the funds to cover up to 75 percent of the cost of work-study salaries. Individual schools finance the remaining balance of the student payroll. Students can apply for the Federal Work Study program by filling out the Free Application for Federal Student Aid (FAFSA). Work-study grants are awarded based on need, but students are urged to apply early for the federal program because of limited funds.

An Anti-Debt Plan

"Work-study programs are an earn-as-you-go opportunity to help students pay for their college education," said Marcia Conliffe, Associate Vice President of Student Success and Enrollment Management Services at Broward Community College. "By earning money to cover their educational expenses, students are not forced to borrow as much in student loans that will need to be repaid after graduation."

When I arrived at Georgetown University in August of 1976, I learned valuable lessons about work-study programs, including the importance of getting an early start on the campus job hunt. The best jobs on campus go quickly, I discovered during my first few weeks as a college student. Between new student orientation, registration, and sightseeing tours of Washington, D.C., my campus job hunt started slowly and the plum positions in the library and academic offices were all taken before I had even filled out my first application. There were, however, plenty of openings in the school cafeteria, which was operated by the catering arm of Marriott Hotels when I was a GU undergrad.

Working in the campus food service department was something of a family tradition. For example, when my mother was a college student in the mid-1950s, she worked in the campus cafeteria to make ends meet. About 20 years later, I reported for work at the school cafeteria, where I dished out hash brown potatoes and quiche. That was my first job, excluding babysitting. I worked eight to 12 hours a week. My salary wasn't much, but my part-time pay covered many of day-to-day expenses during the school term.

I had other jobs during my four years at Georgetown University:

♦ Peer counselor for the Minority Student Affairs program

♦ Summer housekeeping staff (cleaned dorm rooms for salary, and received free room during the summer months)

♦ Writing tutor at the Writing Center

♦ Resident Assistant (dorm floor leader)

I loved my years at Georgetown and every form of employment added a lot to my sense of self, responsibility, and character. What's more, many of the skills that I acquired on campus were invaluable after graduation. Other students also value the experience, contacts, and salary provided from campus employment.

Diapers and exams

As an undergraduate, Lisa Ibanez worked up to 20 hours a week for two years in the infant room at a preschool affiliated with the University of Miami.

"I changed diapers. I gave bottles. I prepared food," recalls Ibanez, who later enrolled in a graduate program at UM.

She enjoyed working with children and appreciated the flexibility of her on-campus assignment, which enabled her to easily shift between classes and work. As a graduate student, she most recently worked on campus as a research assistant and enjoyed the same level of flexibility that she encountered during her undergraduate years. Campus-based employers are also lenient during mid-term and final exam periods and make accommodations during academic crunch periods.

"All of the people knew that we were students first and employees second," said Ibanez.

Mentors and resume perks

Alex Jean-Jacques, a work-study student from Hollywood, Florida, worked six to eight hours a day in his school's financial aid office in downtown Fort Lauderdale.

On a typical Tuesday, for example, he woke up at 4:30 a.m. to lift weights and prepare for an 8:00 a.m. class on campus. By 10, he reported to the financial aid office, where he worked until 4:30 p.m. After a three-hour evening class, Jean-Jacques studied until midnight. It was a long day, but the perks of campus employment extended far beyond the paycheck. Many of the students I chatted with worked second jobs that provided mentors and experience for their resumes in their post-school careers.

"I'm able to learn more and gain more experience, especially while working in an office," said Jean-Jacques, who was studying to be an architect when I met him.

College prep gets a failing grade

Meanwhile, college financial aid pros give students and their families poor grades for college prep. Bad cases of denial are causing more families to lag behind in college savings, according to a new poll of college financial aid administrators from AllianceBernstein Investments.

How bad is it? A 2006 survey showed the families of college-bound students often spend more on annual perks and luxuries than college savings.

♦ 58 percent spend more on restaurants and take-out food

♦ 49 percent spend more on family vacations

♦ 38 percent spend more on electronic gadgets

Thirty-one percent of parents who plan to contribute to their children's education have put more money toward their children's allowance in the past year than they have put in their college savings fund. Almost three-quarters of parents (74 percent) admit they could be saving significantly more for education if they limited money spent on traveling, entertainment, electronics, and impulse purchases.

"Most parents are about as prepared to meet college costs as freshmen are to do their own laundry," said Jennifer DeLong, Director, College Savings Plans, AllianceBernstein Investments, the retail asset management arm of AllianceBernstein L.P. "Parents' poor college savings and investing habits have been exacerbated by grossly unrealistic expectations for financial aid. It is the perfect storm of planning—and if they're not careful, for many families, the result will be a financial shipwreck."

Here's a short summary of other findings:

♦ 72 percent of parents believe their kids will receive scholarships for "special or unique talents."

♦ 97 percent of financial aid administrators polled think that families have a "false sense of security" about financial aid assistance.

♦ 92 percent of financial aid staffers believe that parents overestimate the size of scholarship packages.

Most parents (about 66 percent) believe that their children will graduate from college with debt. The average estimate: about $27,500. But that heavy debt load is bundled with a lot of other financial and emotional baggage.

Debt-delayed adulthood

A survey of college graduates between ages 21 and 35 found that 42 percent felt that they live paycheck to paycheck because of education loans. What's more, 34 percent reported selling belongings in order to cover regular expenses.

Citing the burden of education loans:

♦ 44 percent of graduates (21 -35) have delayed purchasing a home

♦ 28 percent have delayed parenthood

♦ 32 percent have moved in with the folks or have remained home longer than anticipated

There are, however, many solutions for planning for college expenses, according to financial professionals. For instance, investment specialists at Nationwide Financial recommend these steps:

1. Have a family meeting. Talk to your college-bound student about tuition costs and related expenses. Present a realistic snapshot about what you can afford (and are willing to cover).

2. Do your homework. There are many options for scholarships, grants, and educational loans. For example, there are over 2,300 sources of financial aid for education, representing almost $3 billion in funding, according to the College Board.

3. Job hunt. Your college-bound student can find a part-time job that will enable the student to contribute towards college costs. Help and encourage your student to find work.

4. Establish fiscal discipline. Tap into an automatic savings plan, which makes the process of saving feel somewhat painless and predictable. What's more, so-called found money—from birthday checks, tax returns and bonuses—can all be stashed into a college savings account.

5. Get a head start. An early start will expand your menu of options and allow the money in your savings plan to grow and compound over a greater period of time.

Prepaid tuition plans

Not too far from my Dream House there is a smaller home that is owned by one of my closest friends. In the mid-1990s, when they purchased that house—a one floor, three bedroom, two bath home with a large guest room—my friends found one of the last homes on Miami Beach priced under $200,000. Conservatively, that property is now worth close to a $1 million.

My friends have accomplished that same magic with their son's college savings plan. By enrolling in a prepaid tuition plan—also known as a 529 Plan—they purchased four years of education at a steep discount.

A prepaid tuition plan works like this: On a monthly basis, families pay small amounts into a college investment plan through automatic withdrawals from savings or checking accounts. Monthly contributions vary according to state, but in Florida payments are about $25 for tuition in a two-year college and under $82 monthly for a four-year school. Many other states such as Ohio and Alabama have comparable programs.

Once, you have enrolled in the program your payments are fixed at that amount. And when it's time for your student to attend college, the prepaid plan pays tuition, dormitory costs and other fees. In addition, parents, grandparents, relatives, friends, and even business associates can open a college investment prepaid plan. Clearly, the numbers make sense: In 2006, a family of a newborn child could buy four years of college tuition at a public university for about $28,200, compared to the projected cost of $93,628 in 18 years. Program details and savings change from year to year.

Paying for textbooks

During my first semester on campus, I saved money by purchasing used books for my classes. I found two main sources for used books, including the campus bookstore, which had a steady supply of used textbooks that were about 30 percent cheaper than brand-new copies.

I also found great deals buying directly from other students, and got anywhere from 50 to 70 percent off. These bargains were harder to come by and required more work. I had to vigilantly scan handwritten signs and notes that were posted on bulletin boards around campus, and sometimes I was lucky.

Textbook prices have risen dramatically over the last decade. The Public Interest Research Group (PIRG)—a consumer watchdog organization—estimates that school book prices have outstripped the inflation rate for finished goods by nearly 400 percent since 1994. And on an annual basis, students spend roughly $900 a year on textbooks, according to data from PIRG.

To contain costs, many online shopping portals provide great resources for cheaper books, including *www.BestBookBuys.com* and *www.textbookx.com*. These online services enable students and other shoppers to compare prices posted by online and brick-and-mortar stores. The list of vendors ranges from large name-brand heavy hitters to small home-based booksellers. Best Book Buys—an online price comparison portal for books—helps you find school textbooks with average discounts of up to 77 percent for used books and 25 percent for new books.

After tapping into one service, I found the *The Complete Idiot's Guide to Writing Poetry* at a dozen electronic sites. The vendor list included information on shipping costs and condition of the book. The lists ranked prices from cheapest to most expensive and noted which copies were used. There is even a column that rates vendors with links to actual customer comments. That feature is especially helpful for considering independent stores and mom-and-pop sellers.

"You want to know who you are dealing with," said Theresa Smith, a spokeswoman for *www.BestBookBuys.com.*

Here is a partial list of my search results for a cheap copy of *The Complete Idiot's Guide to Writing Poetry:*

- *Half.com:* $9.79 for a used copy, including shipping

- *BarnesandNoble.com:* $20.94 for a new copy, plus shipping

- *Walmart.com* and *Overstock.com*: $13.30 for a new copy, including shipping

"By comparing prices online at Best Book Buys students can quickly determine where to get the best deal on their books. And by shopping early, students can find the best selection of used books that offers the deepest savings possible," according to a statement from Steve Loyola, president and founder of Best Web Buys, the parent company of Best Book Buys.

Tips for Buying Textbooks Online

Request a book list. College professors often post their reading lists on the Internet. Download a copy.

Get a head start. The supply is limited and the best deals go quickly.

Go global. International editions of the same textbook (same publisher and author) are often sold on the international market for up to 72 percent less than the domestic edition.

Track down coupons. Use Internet search engines to track down coupons and promotions for online and traditional stores. Simply type in a store's name and the words "coupon," "discount," or "promotion."

Do your homework. Research the seller's reputation, return policy, shipping charges, and applicable sales tax.

Document your purchase. Print a copy of the confirmation page. This information is handy for tracking a purchase or handling disputes.

Become a seller. When the semester or school year ends, earn extra money by selling your textbooks through online channels. Best Book Buys provides a link to sites seeking used books: *www.bestwebbuys.com/books/buyback.html.* 🌴

Lessons From My First Job

In January of 1981—six months after graduating from Georgetown—I began working for a television station in Pittsburgh, where I was hired to be a news assistant. It was an entry-level position that many college graduates would have killed for, especially in Pittsburgh, which was one of the top ten television markets in the country during the early 1980s. I was very grateful for the job.

It was a foot in the door and I literally needed both feet, plus my Nike track shoes, to keep up with my job. That's because news assistants are the go-fers in the world of journalism. For example, right before the six o'clock broadcast, my main job was to run tapes from the editing rooms into the director's booth.

Sprinting was required because our newsroom was not yet fully automated. And so, about 30 seconds before broadcast, I literally ran down one long hallway, up a flight of stairs, through another hallway and into the broadcast booth, where I handed over a videotape to the engineer on duty. I had prepared for this job during my last two years at Georgetown, where I had started running and had become fast enough to run on the University track team during my senior year. By specializing in sprints and relay races, I was well-prepared for my broadcast career.

I was Joan Cusack—the speedy tape girl—in the 1987 movie *Broadcast News*. Of course, I had other assignments. I wrote the captions that appeared on screen under talking-head news interviews.

Sometimes, I wrote copy for the 10-second news briefs that ran before the late news: Man Dead. Six Shot, Details at 11. It was like writing haiku—a three-line poem constructed from a frugal choice of words.

On good nights, I got to hang out for drinks with the anchormen, reporters, and photographers who all worked the same 4 p.m. to midnight shift. And yes, again, I was very grateful for the job, which paid about $120 a week.

To make ends meet, I lived rent-free on the top floor of my aunt and uncle's home on Elm Street in Wilkinsburg, a small municipality on the outskirts of Pittsburgh. My little suite consisted of a bedroom, walk-in closet and a large sitting room that looked out onto oak, elm and birch trees. There are no palm trees in the northwest corner of Pennsylvania, which is not far from the Appalachian mountains.

My Aunt Norma and Uncle Ike, who offered me their attic apartment, were actually my older cousins on my mother's father's side. My Uncle Ike was a cousin by marriage from a prosperous Black family in Pittsburgh. His mother owned several parcels of property in Pittsburgh and Ike had graduated from Duquesne University in 1949. He also graduated with a law degree from the same university in 1954, while employed with the Internal Revenue Service.

But even with their relative wealth, my aunt and uncle always lived very, very frugally. For example, Aunt Norma was a bulk-buying pioneer. Long before it was fashionable, she used to purchase huge quantities of food and dry goods. As a little girl, I often visited Aunt Norma and Uncle Ike during the 1960s and 1970s, and I have vivid memories of the long white freezer that Aunt Norma kept in the basement of her four-story home in Pittsburgh.

"She was one of the first to have a deep freezer and it stayed loaded," my mom said. After retiring and relocating to the deep pockets of Georgia, my Aunt Norma lived frugally and lived well right up until her recent passing. She clipped coupons, shopped at thrift stores, and gave generously.

How frugal was Aunt Norma?

She found all-you-can-eat buffets with the most food, and she knew the menus of the best buffets by heart, my mom said.

She took full advantage of senior citizen and AAA discounts.

As an interest rate shopper, my aunt was also far ahead of the curve. Back in the day when banks gave away toasters, casserole dishes, and other perks, she shopped around for either the best interest rate or the best gifts whenever she received unexpected financial gifts or faced maturing funds.

She married smart. In an era when African-American college-educated professional males were quite rare, my Aunt Norma married my Uncle Ike, a professional with educational pedigree and a real estate portfolio. Plus, he's a wonderful guy.

Aunt Norma was generous. "She always believed in sharing," my mom said. Like my parents, she always remembered birthdays, anniversaries, and holidays. With Aunt Norma, the check was always in the card; the card always in the mail. And the card arrived on time.

My rent-free life in Pittsburgh ended when my aunt and uncle sold their Elm Street home and relocated to Georgia—returning after decades to our family's southern roots. In preparation for the big move, Aunt Norma sold many of her possessions at a garage sale. She also gave me the sheets, pots, and other items that she no longer needed.

Suddenly, I was in the market for an apartment in Pittsburgh. Once again, the lessons that I learned at Georgetown came to my rescue and

I studied the bulletin boards on area campuses for rental news. At the University of Pittsburgh, I found a notice posted by a female student seeking a roommate to share an off-campus apartment in the Squirrel Hill section of Pittsburgh.

It was an ideal neighborhood. Not only was Squirrel Hill close to the Pitt campus, but it was near the major bus routes that I used to commute to my job at the television station. Additionally, Squirrel Hill was, and still is, the home of a large Orthodox Jewish community in Pittsburgh. My roommate wasn't Jewish, but our landlord was Jewish and many of my neighbors were also of that faith.

I considered myself an expert on that religion because of the Judaic services and events I had attended at different synagogues with my childhood friends in Cherry Hill. I had also learned a little bit about Judaism from my grandmother Julia, the A.M.E. minister. As a housekeeper, she had worked for a Jewish family that she loved. Due to professional and personal interests, Julia learned a lot about Jewish holidays.

One night, maybe two or three years before she died, Julia told me all about Chanukah—the Jewish festival of lights—as it was celebrated in her employer's home. That night, I fell asleep in a twin bed with my grandmother's arms around me and her voice in my ear, telling me her version of Chanukah.

In Pittsburgh, I became further immersed in the Jewish religion and rituals. From a downstairs neighbor, I learned more about the laws and customs of the Jewish Sabbath and about minor holidays. My knowledge and neighborhood contacts aided me professionally, when I had an opportunity to research—with reporter Lynn Cullen—a special news report about the role of Catholic, Protestant, and Jewish women in religion.

For that assignment, I interviewed a woman from my neighborhood, Frumma Rosenberg. Her family included several children, including my future husband, Avi, who was 14 when we first met. Focused on the TV shoot with his mother, I had no contact with him then.

That special report and others helped me to earn a series of promotions and pay raises at the television station. But even with those advances, I was financially struggling and professionally unhappy. It was not a pleasant time to live in Pittsburgh.

In the winter of 1981, the old steel mills were closing and thousands of blue collar workers—many of whom earned handsome salaries—were laid off. Our news reports were filled with tales of loss and depression. After my 4 p.m. to midnight shift, I often went home and cried.

What's more, I wanted to do more than sprint around the newsroom and write copy for other people to read. I wanted to be a six-figure-salary, on-air broadcaster.

Driven by ego and money, I tried to transform myself into an anchor-woman. I took voice lessons. I bought new clothes. I found a hair dresser who could transform my hair (frizzy tight, tight curls) into a shiny straight helmet of hair. But that made-for-TV makeover didn't really work for me. In the world of 1980s Barbie doll anchorwomen, I was a little Bratz doll—not yet ready for prime time.

So I started earning extra money by cleaning a neighbor's home on weekends, writing freelance articles for local and national publications, and even modeling.

The Saks Fifth Avenue retail store in Pittsburgh hired me as a petite model for a few of their in-store runway shows. To save money, I also went to the dollar matinee in Pittsburgh, furnished my apartment with secondhand furniture and purchased books from a used bookstore.

My love of used books—another legacy from my student days—continued in Pittsburgh, where I was a steady customer at the Book Worm, a wonderful used bookstore in Squirrel Hill.

My emerging spendthrift profile

Although, I developed thrifty reading habits in Pittsburgh, I also became a spendthrift. It's tempting to blame my bad spending habits on the hectic newsroom schedule. And indeed, I often worked the evening (4 p.m. to midnight) shift or the overnight shift (4 a.m. to noon). Once, I even worked for almost 24 hours straight—from 3 p.m. until about noon the next day.

With those hours, I ate out for nearly every meal. When I was saving money, I purchased hot-dogs from a man on a street corner near my home or I spent a few bucks for several bags of microwave popcorn.

For mid-priced meals, I ate at local diners, including the local Eat 'n Park on Murray Avenue in Squirrel Hill. And a couple times a week, I ate at upscale restaurants in Shadyside, an elegant shopping district in Pittsburgh.

But I can't honestly pin my bad spending habits on the media or on Pittsburgh. Sure, I was too busy working to cook or shop for groceries. But miraculously, I found time for expensive beauty salon treatments, concerts, and shopping dates. For example, one day when I was modeling for Saks Fifth Avenue, I received a check and an employee shopping discount for the day. I traded my earnings and my one-day shopping pass for a black and white leather Halston purse, which I added to my growing collection of designer merchandise.

The label on the purse should have come with a warning: Danger, you have become an emotional shopper. Unsatisfied with my life and dazed by the culture shock of life after college, I was trying to buy happiness. FD

I Love New York

Restless in the Iron City, I purchased a one-way bus ticket from Pittsburgh to New York City, where I planned to reinvent myself as a poet, novelist, and newspaper journalist. I had mixed feelings about leaving Pittsburgh. My sister Debra had enrolled at the University of Pittsburgh undergrad program. I had a promising job, a cushy, low-rent apartment, and the security of friends and finances in a very affordable city.

In fact, during that period of revitalization Pittsburgh began to score high marks as a livable city due to its affordable housing, wide range of cultural activities and low crime rate. Pittsburgh was listed number one in the top ten list of the most livable cities in America.

I have different theories about why I felt so unhappy in such a great city. Call it post-adolescent trauma. After four years of Marriott-catered cafeteria meals at Georgetown; deadline-friendly, extension-granting professors, and long summer vacations, I was traumatized by the idea of gathering my own food, punching a time clock, and working for 50.5 weeks of a 52-week work calendar. Given my pampered mindset, I don't think that I would have been happy anywhere, not even living on the top floor suite of my Dream House in Miami Beach.

Moving sale

Finally, in May of 1984, after nearly three and a half years in Pittsburgh, I stuffed my possessions into two green duffel bags purchased from an army surplus store. Anything that didn't fit into those bags was either given away or sold at a two-day moving sale on the front porch of the Squirrel Hill house in which I had an attic apartment.

From that moving sale, I earned about $200—maybe less—by selling my furniture, which included a secondhand dresser (sold for $25) and a flip couch and futon double bed that I had purchased new from a discount store for about $150—and re-sold at the moving sale for about $75. The other sale items included lamps, appliances, and the almost-new cast-iron pots that I barely used because I always ate out.

I tried to sell my clothes, especially the wannabe anchorwoman suits with bowties and padded shoulders. But not many people wanted or needed my size-zero power suits or my Cyndi Lauper-inspired collection of off-the-shoulder mini dresses, which looked like something Jennifer Beals wore in the 1983 movie *Flashdance*, coincidentally set in Pittsburgh.

Of course, the Halston bag—my first taste of designer trinkets—came with me. That chain-link clutch bag was precious eye candy from Saks Fifth Avenue and meant a lot to me. But I should have left the designer bag on its high-priced shelf. Not only did the Haltson purse cost a day of modeling fees, plus a chunk of my television salary, the clutch also cost two-weeks pay from my new job in Manhattan as a research assistant for *Editor & Publisher* magazine.

Here's what happened: Shortly after arriving in the big city, I went out to a payday/fun-day lunch date with other members of the research department. Our Friday happy hour began at noon with reservations at a Chinese restaurant on the lower end of Fifth Avenue.

While I chewed on fried wonton noodles dipped in hot mustard and duck sauce, my flashy designer bag dangled from the back of my chair. And sometime between the wonton soup appetizer and the fortune cookie dessert, a thief stole my purse—which also contained my Pennsylvania Driver's License, family photos and a bank envelope stuffed with two-weeks' salary. My co-workers covered my bill and a close friend gave me a $20 loan. Otherwise, I was broke, but wiser.

Lessons from my Halston bag

1. Watch your back. On the street, in the office and in restaurants I've learned to safeguard my possessions and to be mindful of security. Bottom line: Don't make yourself an easy target for thieves.

2. Avoid flashy accessories. To the informed eye, the label on my designer bed screamed: Steal me please. I call it my CCCL Lesson: Conspicuous Consumption Costs Lots.

3. Don't carry around wads of cash. I should have deposited the check directly into my bank or immediately placed the cash into my checking account.

4. Eat brown bag lunches. No meal is worth two-weeks salary. Even a steady diet of crime-free takeout meals can steal away my financial security.

My Takeout Tab				
Sandwich	Daily	Weekly	Monthly	Yearly
Tuna and Pickle	$6.50	$32.50	$130	$1,560
Chicken Breast	$4.00	$20.00	$80	$ 960
Turkey Breast	$6.00	$30.00	$120	$1,440

Compare the daily cost of a homemade lunch ($1.50) to a $5 takeout during the course of 250 workdays. Under that schedule you would save $875 a year by making your own lunch. Over a 10-year period, skipping the $5 daily takeout could generate $11,000, based on a 5 percent annual yield.

Fortunately, I didn't starve after my cash-stuffed purse was stolen.

I also had a steady supply of free restaurant dinners. Thanks to my roommate—my best friend from high school—I found a part-time job in the New York restaurant where she was a waitress.

Over the phone, the restaurant manager eagerly hired me based on my friend's recommendation and my food-service experience. But when I actually showed up to fill out the application, the manager was shocked to see me. And instead of hiring me as a full waitress, she offered me the "runner's spot," which meant that I delivered food to the table, but I didn't take customer orders or earn a full portion of the tip pool.

What's more, I spent a lot of time working in the kitchen with the cooks from Haiti, the Dominican Republic, and Puerto Rico. Repeatedly, I watched as other African-American candidates—very attractive and very well-spoken—were turned away as waiters or waitresses. And through the grapevine, I heard that my experience was not uncommon in the New York restaurant world. Meanwhile, as a runner, I earned a cut of tips, a modest hourly rate and free dinner meals until I found a restaurant that would hire me as a full server.

Extra jobs

The extra income helped cover my share of rent and utilities on the loft-style apartment that I shared with a few other girls in Midtown Manhattan.

In addition to supplementing my meager publishing salary (about $16,000), my restaurant work led to other perks. For example, my restaurant contacts led to shoe-modeling gigs. Manhattan eateries are filled with aspiring actors and models.

While serving burgers and re-stocking condiments, I became friendly with an actress who was also a shoe model. Spotting my size-six feet—the same size as manufacturer sample shoes—she pushed me on the foot trail and gave me the name of her agent. He sent me to go-see appointments with representatives from different major shoe lines. Eventually I was hired by a small California-based company and I modeled their footwear at industry trade shows, which were held in Manhattan hotels over long weekends.

My modeling stint was cut short when I was hired as a financial reporter for the newsletter division of *Institutional Investor* magazine. Due to the higher pay and the longer hours, I hung up my restaurant uniform and put away my go-see modeling head shots. I was a serious financial journalist, and it was the smartest move I ever made.

In May of 1985, when the Dow Jones Industrial Average had not yet broken through the 1,200 mark, CNBC was not yet on the air and financial journalists were in short supply. As such, Tom Lamont—editor in chief of the newsletter division of *Institutional Investor* magazine—was willing to hire novice journalists and train them on the fundamentals of the capital markets. It was a simple lesson plan: You either quickly learned how Wall Street operated or Lamont fired you.

On weekends and evenings, I devoured *Barron's, Forbes, Money*, the *Wall Street Journal* and the business section of *The New York Times*.

I took traders and stockbrokers out for drinks and picked their brain for stock tips, economic insights, and gossip from the financial district. As such, working for *Institutional Investor* was like going to grad school and getting paid to receive an MBA-quality education. But the greatest lessons on money management came from Lamont, our chief, who is a frugal maven. Even his wife Kathy calls him a tightwad.

Saving money at the ballpark

Among all the advice Lamont shared with us, this tip was taken to heart by all of the sports nuts on staff.

"[In 2006,] I saved $1,453 from clipping coupons and signing up at designated driver booths at Giants Stadium, Continental Arena and Shea Stadium. Why pay $4 for a coke when they'll give you one free if you just show a driver's license and promise not to booze it up (which I wouldn't do anyway). Do the math. Fifty games per year multiplied by $8 per game equals $400. That pays for several playoff tickets!"

And most stadiums have such booths. They don't advertise them but if you ask an usher or staff member at an information booth they'll direct you to them.

His thrifty lifestyle has given Lamont extra cash to travel around the globe, own expensive race horses, and provide inner-city children with generous scholarships to private Catholic schools. As a couple, the Lamonts have supported over a dozen underprivileged children with funds for tuition, books, and related expenses.

And Lamont tried to help the rest of us with periodic lectures about our own personal finances. Lamont, for instance, made a big show of walking from his executive office into the kitchen for the free office coffee. But the rest of us made daily and even hourly trips to the Greek coffee shop on the corner or to the high-end café across the street where we purchased cappuccinos and ice coffees years before anyone even heard of Starbucks.

The steam from our costly coffee cups used to make steam come out of Lamont's ears as he railed about the hundreds, maybe thousands of dollars we were spending on coffee. I was a married mom in Miami before I did the math and realized that Lamont was right—I had wasted a ton of money (maybe thousands and thousand of dollars) on coffee.

It all adds up

I figured the costs of my gourmet coffee habits and muffin treats (600 calories!) with the help of Hugh Chou, a systems network administrator at Washington University in St. Louis.

Chou calculates how much our little expenses cost on an annualized basis and how much we would earn if those funds were stashed in a long-term investment account. His free online calculators, (the "Stop Buying Coffee and Save Calculator," the "Lunch Savings Calculator," and the "Gas Guzzling Calculator"), have made Chou a hero in many financial circles. His calculators—dozens of them—are featured on his website, *www.HughChou.org.*

Here's how the coffee calculator works: Based on $3 per day over a typical work year of about 250 days, the calculator figures that your coffee break costs $750 a year. Homemade coffee, Chou calculates, would cost only about 25 cents a day and would save you $687 annually. If you invest that amount in a 6 percent investment vehicle, and continue to do so annually, you would amass $9,420.76 in 10 years.

My love affair with coffee

When my siblings and I walked home from school during the 1960s, my grandmother Julia was often there to greet us. She often provided childcare for me and my siblings, and when Julia was around our kitchen always smelled like coffee. My grandmother brewed hot coffee and then served it with sweetened condensed milk from a short red and white Carnation can. I loved the taste of that sweet thick milk with a little of the coffee that was left in her saucer.

As such, my life-long love affair of coffee began when I was six or seven. I loved the taste because I loved my grandmother. So it's no surprise that as an adult, I became a big fan of Starbucks and high-end coffee shops. I like Starbucks. I like the luxury and atmosphere of cafes that offer lattes made just for me. Those are my periodic treats.

But day in and day out, I love the coffee that we make at home. In fact, it actually tastes far better than lattes from the cafes, and just as good as the authentic Cuban coffee shops in Miami. I estimate that our rich homemade coffee saves us about $1,200 every year.

A coffee recipe that saves thousands

The ingredients:

Whole beans. Forget the gourmet beans. Eight O' Clock coffee beans are super cheap and earned top marks for flavor in a blind taste test from *Consumer Reports*.

Grind the beans as needed. Every morning with our bean crusher, we grind coffee beans into a fine powder. The aroma of freshly ground beans creates the ambiance of a cafe. The scent also reminds me of my grandmother.

Pre-ground shortcut. When pressed for time we grind beans in advance and store them. This shortcut helps on super crazy mornings.

Water. Filtered tap water makes yummy coffee. This step makes a big difference, especially if the water from your tap has a strong taste.

Spices. For an extra kick, grind the coffee beans with either a little bit of cardamom, cinnamon, or vanilla beans. This adds flavor and it's not hard to throw in a little bit of spice during the grinding process.

Cream. I love half-and-half in my coffee. There are cheaper solutions with fewer calories. But I enjoy this luxury.

The equipment:

We don't use fancy or expensive equipment. Our low-tech coffee production gear is low-cost, effective, and pretty. Experts agree with our strategy.

The bean crusher. We spent $20 to $30. This grinder also works on spices.

The plunger pot. Also known as a French press coffee-maker. We spent about $14, marked down from $40.

Beautiful mugs. We've spent 50 cents to $10 for mugs.

Coffee with our French press pot:

1. Boil about a teapot full of filtered tap water.
2. Crush about two fistfuls of coffee beans, include powdered cinnamon or cardamom beans.
3. Place the ground coffee into the plunger pot.
4. Fill the pot with 16 to 18 ounces of boiled water. Let the hot mixture sit for five minutes.
5. Press the plunger down, a simple motion that filters the coffee and separates the grinds.
6. Serve coffee in ceramic mugs with cream, sugar, or other spices.

In the book, *The Joy of Coffee*, writer Corby Kummer makes a big pitch for elegant, but frugal coffee equipment. In his chapter, "Low-Tech Solution," the author writes:

"Before you take out a loan, consider the coffee-making method that has been popular in Italy for more than half a century—one that will require a layout of less than $30."

He refers to Moka stovetop brewers, which are widely used in Italy. We've recently tried this coffee stovetop pot (purchased for under $20), and we've been pleased with the rich coffee and the low-cost.

Quality at the drugstore

Expensive coffee wasn't my only bad indulgence. As an insecure, unmarried, twenty-something woman in Manhattan I obsessed about my appearance. From manicures to day spa facials, I spent at least $500 each month on nails, hair, and cosmetics. But when it comes to cosmetics, high cost does not always equal high-quality care.

"There are very good products at CVS and Walgreens that are very effective and very affordable," said Dr. Helena Igra, a cosmetic surgeon and board-certified dermatologist from Miami Beach. "The most expensive products are not necessarily the best."

So there's no need to feel deprived if you can't afford to spend hundreds of dollars a month on skincare products. Nor should you feel compelled to purchase the high-end, over-the-counter skincare products that some dermatologists market directly to their patients, said Igra, who does not sell skincare products in her office. Indeed, she's happy to suggest a number of "very good, very dependable" drugstore products—from publicly traded household names—that will pamper your skin at a fraction of the costs.

Of course, if you have serious skin problems, prescription-only pharmaceutical intervention may be necessary. But many of the inexpensive, over-the-counter products work just fine for the everyday nuisances wrought by sun and stress (fine lines, small eruptions, and brown spots), Igra said.

And while, some expensive skin-care products live up to their billing, packaging, research and development costs and marketing budgets can also boost lofty price tags, the doctor said.

That same lesson was personally delivered to me by a television talk show host, who discovered the beauty of pharmacy cosmetics after losing her luggage—including a bag of expensive cosmetics—while traveling. In a pinch, she purchased inexpensive cosmetics at a pharmacy counter and was pleased with the results. Other women in corporate circles have shared similar discoveries with me.

Stephen Farrar, a television and video makeup artist, agrees. As a beauty industry professional, he has peeked into the makeup kits of peers from around the country. Their tools of the trade typically include many inexpensive cosmetic products, including Max Factor, Almay, CoverGirl, and Maybelline, Farrar said. In fact, when it comes to mascara, the old pink and green Maybelline mascara wand ($4.99) ranks as an industry staple.

"It doesn't have to cost a lot to look good," said Farrar.

And if you're addicted to one of the expensive department store or designer brands, enjoy. But learn to streamline and shop for value, the makeup artist added.

"There are some good products at the high-end of the market, but you don't have to buy the whole line," Farrar said.

Spa chat: $250 manicure and cheap polish

Ten painted, clipped and massaged fingers—at $25 each. That's a total of $250 for a manicure at a high-end New York salon, according to an article in *People* magazine. But there are far cheaper alternatives.

1. Beauty schools. For about $5 or 50 cents a finger, manicures are available at many beauty schools. I have also received cheap, cheap haircuts and hair treatments at different beauty schools, and have been pleased with the price and the results. But caution: play the look-see game first. Not all students are created equally. Look at finished products before sitting down in anyone's chair.

2. You do it. With simple kits from the drugstore, Do-It-Yourself French manicures cost as low as 50 cents (or less) per session. That's a nickel a finger.

3. Polish already dried. Avon has a dry paint manicure. It's like applying thin paint chips to your nails. The manicure looks very professional and lasts up to two weeks. (I've tried it.) The prices for this product range from about $5 to $8. It's easy and cheap. And you don't have to wait for your nails to dry. No smearing.

4. Clearly cheap. Just slap on a coat of clear polish for pennies a session. It looks great. It's cheap and when the paint inevitably chips, no one notices because the gloss is colorless.

5. In the buff. Or just buff your nails with a good nail brush. Apply olive oil to your cuticles. The process provides a natural gleam without the harsh chemicals.

Cheap Entertainment in NYC

I'm not sure why I spent so much money in Manhattan. Maybe a broken wedding engagement, unsuccessful attempts to write the Great

American Novel, and the constant press of high debt prompted me to spend even more.

Like a character in Tama Janowitz's 1986 novel, I was one of the *Slaves of New York*. I rented summer vacation shares in the Hamptons—where Steven Spielberg, Martha Stewart, and the financial titans of Wall Street had luxurious summer homes—and I went to Europe twice. I had no money, but I always had Paris, where I stayed with friends who lived and worked in the City of Lights. I had a charmed life.

Fortunately, I also developed a wide repertoire of frugal habits and I learned to enjoy the free or low-cost entertainment that is available in New York City. Taking advantage of entertainment deals in New York City made it so I've looked for deals in every city I've lived since then. The free and low cost entertainment opportunities are amazing.

Staten Island Ferry. When I lived in Manhattan, the Staten Island Ferry was 25 cents for a great ride. (The private cruises are lots more.) Now the ferry is free and you catch a glimpse of the Statue of Liberty during the ride.

Street Performers. Check out Central Park, Washington Square Park and Union Square Park. On the streets and in the parks, you can watch extreme skaters, dancers, musicians, singers, and little girls jumping Double Dutch at heart-breaking, breath-taking speed.

Free spectator basketball games. In New York there are some highly competitive pickup games that are great to watch. The Fourth Street basketball courts in the West Village is my favorite spot to watch skilled street ball.

Free summer concerts. Concerts take place at Central Park and other locations throughout the city.

Shakespeare in the Park. These productions at The Delacorte Theater in Central Park from the Public Theater in New York (*www.public theater.org*) offer an all-star lineup of Hollywood and Broadway stars. The various productions that I have seen were hip, funky, or traditional, but all were excellent. What's more, the tickets are free.

Jazz sessions at Dan Lynch Blues Bar in the East Village. In between weekend gigs, many professional musicians in Manhattan show up for free jazz jam sessions on Sunday afternoons. Some of my happiest afternoons have been spent listening to music at Dan Lynch, located at 221 Second Avenue.

Cappuccino at Caffé Reggio in the Greenwich Village. With a cup of coffee, you can sit for hours at this café and people-watch in the Village. This place, at 119 MacDougal Street, has been around since 1927. You'll forget that Starbucks ever existed.

Coney Island Boardwalk. It's free and fun for all ages.

Museums. Brooklyn Museum, Museum of Modern Art, Metropolitan Museum of Art, and art galleries, especially in SoHo.

Discount show tickets. Broadway and off-Broadway shows from the Theatre Development Fund, (*www.tdf.org*).

New and Cheap Books

Reading was also a source of frugal entertainment that I enjoyed while living in New York City, and still is to this day. I enjoyed finding used and unusual books at the Strand Bookstore located at 828 Broadway in lower Manhattan.

I have discovered over my years of searching that discount books—new and gently used—are stocked in unusual places. At the library, for example, I have stumbled upon book sales, where new and slightly worn books started at 50 cents, far less than my family has paid for library late fees. We have also found great book sales at a public tropical garden, a hospital, and retail bookstores.

Hefty discounts

The publishing world is filled with overstocked books and complimentary review copies. These texts are donated to libraries or sold at steep discounts as fundraisers for community groups and charities. For consumers, overstocked book sales translate into big savings.

One visit to a neighborhood branch yielded quite a find. Under the title "Friends of the Library," I found a rack of sale books with a diverse selection of popular fiction, romance, nonfiction bestsellers, and classic texts in new or almost-new condition. Hardbacks were $2 each; paperbacks, between 50 cents and $1.

Sale racks in chain stores

And don't overlook the discount racks at various stores. I have friends who have found great deals on bestselling books at some of the big-box retail chains. My family has also purchased new books for $2 each at red-ticket sales at Barnes & Noble. For example, *The Hemingway Book Club of Kosovo* by Paula Huntley, was originally priced at $21, marked down to $4.98, and finally priced at $1.99 in a post-holiday sale. Borders and Books & Books (a Florida chain) also have great deals on their sale rack.

"We have regular customers who walk straight to the sale rack," one bookstore manager told me.

Sale racks are typically stocked with an oversupply of once-hot sellers or hardback copies of books that will soon be coming out in paperback. On a sale aisle, I have purchased new books for as little as $1 and found $24.95 hardback copies marked down to $6.99.

Book shares

With the help of family, friends, and a former librarian, my friend Lisa Arhart keeps a lot of books in circulation. Arhart, an English professor and a mother of three, loves books and saves literary dollars by checking out the books of others. Operating through a tight network of connections, Arhart swaps and samples books.

Consider the path of her copy of *Harry Potter and the Order of the Phoenix* (book five in J.K. Rowling's series). Arhart stayed up all night to read that book and then passed it to her teenage daughter. When her daughter finished the book, it went to Arhart's mother and then to another teenager.

"By the time we were done, the book had passed through four or five different pairs of hands," said Arhart, who also operates a book exchange with a former librarian.

Arhart is part of a literary movement that goes beyond simply frequenting the public library. Among the free or low-cost options for books and textbooks are informal book-trading clubs, Internet-driven book swaps or online book comparison portals.

Other frugal literary paths include BookCrossings (*www.bookcross ings.com*), a program designed to help "release" books into wider circulation. There are two basic styles of releasing a book:

1. Conservative book owners typically release books to a tight circle, which could include friends, associates, or even a local charity.

2. Adventurous "BookCrossers" release or abandon their books—often marked "free"—in public places such as theaters, park benches, and coffee shops. Those who stumble upon those books are encouraged to follow the instructions on the label and contribute to an online entry. The original book owner can track the path and reception of a book released through Bookcrossings. Book recipients are encouraged to record their book reviews in an online journal at *www.BookCrossings.com*.

"I guess you could say it's the karma of literature," Ron Hornbaker, co-founder, said in a prepared statement. "Releasing your books into the wild and tracking their progress and the lives they touch is just more fascinating and more fulfilling than hoarding them on a shelf somewhere." FD

My Big Fat
Central Park Wedding

In February of 1990, my husband and I started dating. At that time, Avi was 21; I was 31. We weren't really strangers. We'd met seven years earlier when I was part of the news team that had invaded the Rosenbergs' Pittsburgh home to interview Frumma Rosenberg—Avi's mother—for a television news story about religion. In that frame, Avi was a teenage boy in a background shot, and I was a behind-the-scenes producer.

We never spoke.

Our second meeting took place at the Park Avenue apartment of Rabbi Joel Kinney. Separately, Avi and I had received invitations to join a large group of singles celebrating the weekly Friday night rituals associated with Shabbas, the Jewish Sabbath. When we met at that dinner party—both unaware of our mutual connection through his mother—I had been observing Shabbas and keeping Kosher for almost two years.

The third meeting took place the following Saturday morning (about 12 hours after the Friday night dinner party) at the Young Israel Synagogue near Fifth Avenue in lower Manhattan. Standing in the women's balcony, I looked into the main sanctuary and saw Avi holding a Torah scroll. Clearly, a lot had changed since we first met in Pittsburgh. Avi had grown up, and I was living the life of an Observant Jew.

Since childhood, I've been fascinated with Judaism—another interest I shared with my Grandmother Julia, the preacher. I loved my grandmother's church—the people, the pews, and the gospel music that made my heart rock like Noah's ark.

And I love the celebrations of Christmas and Easter in my parents' home. Those family rituals were cherished, warm, and comfortable.

But long before I had any Jewish friends, I had fallen in love with Judaism. It was love at first sight when I was about six or seven and seated alone in my undershirt in the yellow bedroom in the back of the house on the second floor in Philadelphia. The television was on; the lights were off.

The blue-gray light from our small black-and-white set hit three of the four walls in the room and seemed to pull me into the tube. I moved closer to the TV set because I recognized something on that screen.

There was a mountain. There were crowds of people huddled around the mountain. There was a man. I remembered that mountain. I remembered that crowd. I knew that man.

He was Moses and he spoke to G-d on that mountain. Of course, later as an adult, I would google and search for clues about that movie, discovering that I had watched Charlton Heston in *The Ten Commandments*. The movie hit theaters in 1956 and was re-broadcast on the small screen in the mid 1960s as a Sunday night movie of the week.

Later, when I was 9 or 10 and living in the suburbs, I enjoyed hearing a friend read her after-school Hebrew lessons aloud. I didn't understand the words, but they spoke to me. As a teenager, I owned a small gold *Chai*—a Hebrew symbol for life—which I periodically wore around my neck, but under my clothes. And in my late teens or early 20s, I made myself a secret promise: When I was an old lady and about to die, I would find a rabbi and ask him to grant me a final wish: Make me Jewish before I die.

But I didn't wait that long. In my late 20s, a series of self-inflicted emotional, professional, and financial meltdowns emptied all of my accounts and left me feeling spiritually bankrupt. I felt like a triple-layer, bottom-line failure.

Financially. I had nothing but debt to my name. While friends from high school and college were either married with kids or homeowners, I was still living in a loft with a changing cast of roommates arranged through *Village Voice* ads.

Emotionally. Still reeling from a major romantic disappointment from my late teens, I broke other hearts and promises. I was like Julia Roberts' character in the 1999 film *The Runaway Bride*, but my real-life version was not a comedy.

Professionally. In my drive to write the Great American Novel—a Black Princess version of Jay Mcinerney's *Bright Lights, Big City* from 1984—I tossed away other career opportunities as if I were sorting dirty laundry. Even my lucrative and instructive stint at *Institutional Investor* was interrupted by an unpaid, unscheduled year-long leave of absence when I worked in a bookstore, hung out in the Hamptons and went to Europe to research and write my Princess Novel. I financed my creative sabbatical with credit, retirement savings, and air.

As a trendy New Yorker, I tried therapy and it was great. I got to talk and talk. Those gab sessions were like manna from heaven for a young woman called "Chatty Cathy" as a toddler. And at $65 an hour, I found a frugal therapy deal. I even saved money by walking to my therapist's office. Unfortunately, I also spent money—lots of money—after discovering a lovely secondhand furniture store on my walking route.

My Meltdown Furniture Shopping Spree

♦ Oak bookcase, painted-yellow: $30

♦ Antique desk/dressing table: $600

- ◆ Tall mahogany bookcase and cabinet: $250
- ◆ Two stuffed silk chairs: $150
- ◆ Two nightstand tables: $50

There were other purchases, and most of my Manhattan therapy furniture has followed me to Miami. It's a stunning collection and I didn't buy it all at once. On an erratic installment plan (my personal cash leak), I paid for my purchases drip by drip. In fact, the more I cried during therapy, the more I spent later. It was an un-merry-go-round of spending.

The therapy sessions were great (cathartic, insightful, instructional), but I became tired of hearing my own voice and being broke. And finally, you could say, G-d saved me money.

Make me Jewish before I die

Through a fellow reporter at *Institutional Investor*—another girl like me—I found an Orthodox rabbi in the Flatbush section of Brooklyn—Rabbi Meir Fund—and I began taking classes and reading books about religion, mysticism, and Jewish laws.

During one class, Rabbi Fund made a statement that balanced all of my accounts: "What G-d intended for you, no one can take away. And what's not intended for you, you don't need." There were other AHA! Moments, but those words went straight to my bottom line. Basically, I was okay as is—and no amount of spending was a) going to make me a better person or b) make me like myself more.

I had learned those lessons during childhood from my parents, but in the tidal wave of adulthood, my common sense had drifted away. And in an odd sort of way, my studies of Jewish laws and customs carried me back home to myself.

My conversion studies led me to that Shabbat meal where Avi was seated at the same table. During our chance meetings, something clicked between us. Later that weekend, we went out on our first date, and shortly thereafter, fell in love.

We were married in June of 1992 under a chuppah (a wedding

canopy) at Shakespeare Garden in Central Park in Manhattan, complete with a horse-drawn carriage.

After all of the money I had spent and charged on plastic, I was determined to be frugal while planning our wedding. We still spent a lot to have an elegant wedding in Manhattan. (It was even featured in the *New York Times*.) But our expenses were far less than the tab of most New York weddings.

Money-Saving Wedding Tips

Flowers. My bouquet and the flowers for the wedding were picked from a friend's upstate New York home.

Limo. My husband and I took a horse and carriage to and from the wedding. (No gas, no limo.) The rental fee was far less than hiring a stretch limo and a driver.

Location. We found a frugal site for the wedding service. Reserving the Shakespeare Garden in Central Park cost $250 for the government park fee. Other frugal locations for weddings, parties, and other events include office building lobbies, nightclubs (ideal for day time or early evening weddings when nightclubs are closed to the public), municipal gardens, theaters, and party rooms in upscale condo buildings.

Photography. Deborah G., my best friend from high school and a professional photographer, took pictures as her gift to us. Other photographers who attended the wedding also gave us copies of their photos.

Wedding dress. I wore a used gown (my sister's dress).

How does a real Duchess recycle a Royal wedding dress that she'll wear only once? Apparently that question ran through the mind of the Duchess of Cornwall—Camilla—who, when photographed wearing her wedding dress, the British newspapers called her the "Royal Recycler."

"...the Duchess of Cornwall obviously couldn't bear to confine her beautiful wedding outfit to the back of the wardrobe. The royal recycler wore the ivory-hued Robinson Valentine ensemble again this week as she attended the opening of the National Assembly of Wales with her husband," reported *Hello* magazine on June 6, 2007. The Duchess recycled her dress with new accessories, including a different hat and pearls.

There are other ways to recycle a wedding dress:

1. Donate the dress to charity.

2. Create a wedding dress bank. In my community, various women maintain a stock of wedding dresses. It's like a lending library and the formal dress bank is filled with gowns for brides, mothers of the bride, and bridesmaids. This free dress lending service was designed so that brides on a limited budget could look and feel like a million bucks. But the wedding dress library also cuts down on wedding costs and creates a real sense of community. And each dress looks different on every girl or woman. I've gone to lots of local weddings and I've never spotted a familiar-looking dress.

3. Give it to your sister, cousin, or daughter. I wore a hand-me-down gown from one of my younger sisters. It was an expensive dress, but I only spent about $150 on alterations and cleaning. Beyond my immediate family, no one—at least until now—realized that my gown was a repeat performer.

4. Sell the dress on eBay. Or in a consignment store, or through a standard newspaper classified ad.

5. Alter the dress and wear it again. Wear your wedding dress—done over, shortened or re-accessorized—to a black-tie event.

Nationwide, the average couple spends about $27,000 on a wedding. And many newlyweds face years of debt in an effort to pay for rings, The Dress, floral arrangements, the reception, honeymoon and related costs. Those figures can spike almost 50 percent higher if you finance wedding expenses with credit.

A Lengthy Financial Engagement

Credit-Card purchases:	$10,000
Interest rate:	18 percent
Monthly Payment:	Minimum
Total interest costs:	$14,000
Time to repay:	31 years

Thrifty wedding planning tips from CCCS

"Having a dream wedding can result in a financial nightmare for couples who spend more than they can realistically afford," said Jessica Cecere, president of Consumer Credit Counseling Service of Palm Beach County and the Treasure Coast (CCCS). "The financial strain can take a toll on the best of relationships, and can significantly reduce the chances of a successful marriage."

Establish a Spending Plan. How much can you afford on a cash-only basis? Outline how much each partner and their families can afford to contribute. For planning help, *www.eventageous.com* provides a helpful financial worksheet and event checklist.

Create Priorities. What matters most to you and your partner? What are your top priorities? A high-fashion wedding gown? A live band? An elaborate wedding? An awesome honeymoon? Rank each element and allocate money with your priorities in mind.

Buy an eraser. Rub out or cut expenses in areas that matter less. Flowers, wedding programs, and transportation are just a few of the areas where you can cut back.

Wed off-season. Most weddings take place in the summer (June through August) and it costs more to book caterers and halls during that peak season. Save money and increase your negotiating power by getting married during the off-season. It's also cheaper to get married on Sundays and weeknights. And look for holiday seasonal decorating perks: Many hotels, churches, synagogues, and community centers are already decorated for the holidays and will require fewer added ornamental touches for your wedding party.

Opt for self-employment. Do-it-yourself floral arrangements, invitations, wedding favors, and invitations can save lots of money. For ideas check out: *www.allweddingideas.com* and *www.superweddings.com*.

Decorating dos and don'ts

For advice about frugal but elegant floral arrangements, I turned to Richard David, co-owner of "Mark's Garden," a Los Angeles-based retail flower and design shop. The company supplied the centerpieces for the 2005 Academy Awards Governor's Ball and also created floral designs for Jennifer Lopez, Jessica Simpson, Shaquille O'Neal, and other celebrities. We had a fun phone conversation. His advice:

Check out your own backyard. aHomegrown flowers, herbs, vines and greenery can be used to enhance or stretch bouquets purchased from floral shops or supermarkets.

"Just walk around and be creative," David said. "Sometimes, even weeds can be pretty when you add them to flowers."

Be creative. At a recent party, my friend Leah decorated banquet tables with banana leaves. Draped over the tablecloth, the large green leaves provided an elegant, but unusual flourish to the serving tables.

Don't be contained by vases. Teapots, bowls, cups, and other interesting containers provide visual sparks at parties.

Size doesn't matter. Smaller arrangements provide greater flexibility and facilitate conversation. Fruits, berries, and rose petals are also creative but inexpensive materials for decorating tables. "Always remember candles," David said. "Little votive candles always add something to a table arrangement. Flickering lights create a warm and inviting ambiance."

Potted plants are also an option. Indeed, for a recent family function, my husband purchased trays of inexpensive yellow and purple annual flowers from Home Depot. The trays were wrapped in festive tissue paper and provided an elegant touch to the tables. After the party, we planted the flowers in our small garden and gave the rest away.

Newlyweds in Manhattan

As newlyweds, my husband and I lived on the Upper West Side of Manhattan on the third floor of an early 1900s building at 82nd Street and Broadway—not far from Central Park. We paid $1,180 a month for a three-room apartment, and by New York standards that was a real bargain.

Our eldest son Tali was born days before our first anniversary and we welcomed his arrival with a great deal of celebration. He was the first grandchild on both sides of the family, and he was a very happy baby. But we quickly discovered that our dream apartment—a walkup in a non-elevator building—was a kid-care nightmare.

When the baby fell asleep during an outing, my husband and I carried the sleeping child in his Combi stroller up, step by step, as if we were servants lifting nobility in a sedan chair or hauling a Rickshaw cab. Staring at the baby's serene, but transported face, I finally understood the full weight of parenthood.

"Avi," I said as we climbed step after step. "We are slaves for life."

I enjoyed motherhood, including the play dates at Riverside Park and the free storytelling events (with characters) for toddlers at the new Barnes & Noble superstore on Broadway.

Meanwhile, as a working mother, I remained on staff at the newsletter division at *Institutional Investor*, where I had been promoted to managing editor of *Corporate Financing Week*, a publication dedicated to the banking industry.

In my new position, I learned plenty about banking fees, loan rates and borrowing standards—helpful insights for a newlywed. Additionally, I earned a handsome salary with great health benefits, a 401(k) plan, a standard pension, and a flexible salary. But the costs of a full-time nanny, diapers, housing, and other expenses—especially in Manhattan—consumed our income.

What's more, we quickly outgrew our three-room, one-bedroom apartment and needed more space. But even during the recession of the early 90s, larger apartments in Manhattan, Brooklyn, and even in nearby Hoboken, New Jersey, were going for at least $1,500 a month or higher. My husband and I faced the fiscal truth: We couldn't afford to stay in Manhattan.

We wanted to relocate to an affordable, hip and child-friendly city, with a vibrant religious community of synagogues and kosher restaurants. And after a brutal winter in New York, we also wanted to live someplace sunny and warm. Miami—with its tropical mix of cultures—fit that bill. 🌴

Married with Children
in South Beach

Part 1: Financial Lessons for Kids

South Beach, dubbed "Soho in the Sun" by the New York media, was just moving into the national spotlight during the early 1990s. With the revitalization of the Art Deco District—built in the 1920s and 1930s—Miami Beach attracted models, artists, and movie and television production crews. Rent was cheap, housing was available, and synagogues were plentiful.

I found a well-paid job as a banking reporter for a regional business publication—the *Miami Daily Business Review*—and my husband enrolled in an interior design program at the International Fine Arts College in downtown Miami. My new job even covered moving expenses.

We loved our new home, which was a bargain: $800 a month for half a house and a large backyard, complete with a swing-set that reminded me of the jungle gym my father had installed on our back lawn in South Jersey.

But when our landlord put that property on the market, we were forced to re-locate and were lucky to find an opening in the apartment building in which we now live. Our current home is an 1,800 square foot apartment with three bedrooms, and two bathrooms—ample space for our family, which grew to include three children and several pets.

Raising Fiscally-Responsible Kids

Finding an affordable physical living space for my family was easy. However, finding an affordable fiscal niche was more of a challenge, especially in our consumer-driven economy.

Shopping with kids at yard sales or traditional stores is a challenge and the difficulties involve more than just bargain hunting. For example, as I load up my shopping cart, I often wonder what messages I'm sending my children and what sort of messages kids are picking out of the electronic airwaves. Indeed, there's a $16 billion annual push to turn our kids into spending machines.

"We're raising a generation of hyper consumers. This leads to strife within families and a host of behavioral and psychological problems," said Monique Tilford, deputy director the Center for a New American Dream, a consumer watchdog organization based in Maryland.

Children and the media

The average child in the U.S. watches over 100 commercials each day, or over 40,000 television commercials annually. Advertisers now spend over $16 billion each year—up over 250 percent since 1992—in marketing pitches aimed at children, according to the Center for a New American Dream.

And multi-tasking, tech-savvy students, ages eight through 18, are exposed to 8.5 hours of media each day, which exceeds the amount of the time spent in classrooms, according to data from the Kaiser Family Foundation, a nonprofit health policy organization.

Children are not only watching more television. They are also tuned into programs that feature adult content or material that is not age-appropriate, said Dr. Lee Sanders, a pediatrician and an associate professor of pediatrics at the University of Miami's Miller School of Medicine. And in some homes babies and toddlers are exposed to hours of television. About 40 percent of three-month-old babies watch either standard television or DVD recordings, according to a study funded by the National Institute of Mental Health and the Tamaki Foundation. But that early exposure to television (ages three and under) has been linked to the development of attention-deficit with hyperactivity disorder and other learning disabilities.

To limit or avoid the harmful side effects of television, Dr. Sanders recommends several steps. His first prescription: Remove televisions from children's bedrooms.

Now found in at least 50 percent of the bedrooms for children ages two and older, television sets represent a health risk, Sanders said. For instance, medical studies indicate that children with a television in their bedroom are more likely to be obese.

Sanders recommends "co-watching" a strategy in which parents view television programs with their kids and provide critical commentary about content, advertising, and implied messages in shows and commercials. Co-watching can help to avoid nightmares and can reduce the clamor for "as-seen-on-TV" merchandise.

Cutting the electronic cord

1. Limit television viewing with TV-free hours or evenings.

2. Restrict viewing to commercial-free programs or videos.

3. Monitor the time and quality of Internet screen time.

4. Don't let kids watch television alone.

5. Provide commentary about the values, behavior, and products promoted on commercials and shows.

6. Find low-tech alternatives: board games, books, cooking activities, nature walks, and family fitness exercises.

Birthday cake lesson

Do you ever wonder if lessons on saving and spending penetrate the Gameboy heads of your kids? I do. But recently, I spotted major progress.

My middle son, Gabriel, (age 13) is the big spender in the family. He has earned money as a mother's helper and loves to spend cash.

To celebrate the birthday of one of his little charges, Gabriel baked a cake. A store cake would have cost about $15 in our neighborhood. But the box mix and the fancy icing cost only about 4 bucks. And for the candles, he wanted a fancy number 7 candle ($4) and a set of sparkle candles ($4). He was a bit miffed at the high prices for candles. He walked over to the ice cream aisle where similar candles were on sale for only 79 cents each.

The cheaper set looked slightly different than the expensive set, but my son was sold. What's more, after returning from the supermarket, my son proudly boasted about his savings. His smile was as bright as the candles.

Expensive Cake Option	
Item	Cost
Store Cake	$15.00
Fancy #7 Candle	$4.00
Sparkle Candles	$4.00
Total	$29.00

My Son's Cheaper Option	
Item	Cost
Baked Cake	$4.00
Sale #7 Candle	$0.79
Sparkle Candles	$0.79
Total	$5.58

"Smart! aren't I?!" Gabriel said. Lesson learned.

The coupon family lesson plan

On a recent shopping trip, coupons made a big dent in our bill. Using a combination of advertised in-store discounts ($17.55) and coupons ($9.59), my husband saved $27.14, roughly half of our total bill of $56.46.

We"re not the only coupon clippers. U.S. consumers save about $3 billion a year with grocery store coupons, according to the Promotion Marketing Association. Those savings are significant in the current economic climate, according to Manuel Lasaga, president of Strategic Information Analysis, an economic and financial consulting firm. "Coupons can help reduce the gap between what consumers earn and the rising cost of living," Lasaga said.

Coupons are also a useful tool for educating kids about finance and organization. Charles Brown, co-chairman of the Coupon Council at PMA, said he has "used coupons to turn everyday shopping trips with my twins into great learning experiences and quality time spent together."

♦ Couponing with kids. Build educational skills while saving money. Encourage kids to sharpen their organizational skills by arranging coupons by expiration date, category or store. Shoppers who spend 20 minutes a week organizing coupons can shave their annual food bill by 20 percent, according to industry data.

♦ Although 90 percent of coupons are bundled with the Sunday newspaper, manufacturers increasingly use the Internet to publish discounts. Parents can work with kids to use Web-based search engines to track down deals on toys, equipment, entertainment, and food.

♦ For younger children, coupons provide games in number recognition, counting, and simple computations. For older kids, coupons can be used to calculate percentages and multiplication.

♦ Involve kids in planning a family menu. Provide a fixed dollar amount, coupons, and a blank page. Encourage kids to design a menu that fits the dollar limits. A friend tried this with her teenage daughter and was surprised at how strict her daughter became when faced with the chore of managing the family food budget. By the way, it really helps if you offer kids a small cut of the savings. That strategy has worked for me.

My Teen's First Paid Haircut: Finding His Own Frugal Path

For years my husband has given our sons at-home haircuts. In fact, we've been proud of our DIY haircuts and styling efforts. Our hair clippers have saved us thousands of dollars. How do we know this? Trial and big error. When my middle son was three years old, his mix of curly, wavy and straight hair confounded us. So we took our toddler to a hair salon. The cost: $40 for the haircut. Ouch! We paid the bill, tipped well, but have avoided hair salons since then.

Recently, my oldest son decided to take the hair-grooming business into his own hands. He went to Lincoln Road Mall—a trendy outdoor pedestrian mall in South Beach. This shopping district is popular with supermodels, tourists, and spend-happy consumers. (Starbucks has three or four outlets on Lincoln Road.) There are several beauty salons and upscale day spas on or near Lincoln Road. The main hair man for Jennifer Lopez has a salon in the area. Prices are not cheap.

While working on a Mother's Day magazine article, I once enjoyed a manicure and a pedicure at an upscale salon on Lincoln Road. The price tag: $135 to have my nails trimmed, filed, and painted. It was a tough assignment!

So when my teen stepped out for his new Lincoln Road haircut, I was worried. But he arrived home with a close cut, and I was very impressed with the price tag: $14. Skipping past the high-end salons, my son had found an old-school mom and pop barber in one of the ungentrified areas of Lincoln Road.

The bad news: His hair grows fast and maintenance could be a biweekly cash drain.

The good news: He's back to DIY home haircuts. His father just follows the lines of the professional barber, as my son suggested. Lesson learned.

Kids and part-time jobs

It's never too early to teach kids the ABCs of money management, according to experts. "Money management skills are learned by examples that are set from parents, as well as through practice," according to Mike Sullivan, director of education for Take Charge America, a non-profit credit counseling company. "Helping kids build money management skills can prevent them from falling into debt later in life."

How important are summer and part-time jobs to the financial education of kids? Very important, and some celebrity parents agree. According to *TMZ.com*, a popular celebrity blog owned by *Time Warner*, Scout, the daughter of Bruce Willis and Demi Moore had a job. Although the report didn't list the reasons for Scout's job, part-time jobs for kids aren't all about the money.

Summer and part-time jobs offer valuable lessons about discipline, frugal living, organization, and other real-life lessons. Those jobs also provide easy lessons on personal finance.

During a past summer, my boys both had summer jobs. My oldest worked at a pizza store, where he picked up lessons on deadlines, multi-tasking, and math from working at the cash register.

At age 11, my younger son was a mother's helper for a woman with three active children under the age of three. Wow. He came home every night exhausted, but wealthier. The boys also went to camp and on a summer cruise with my parents. Bottom line: They had fun and really learned a lot from their summer jobs.

Kids and cell phones

Haircuts are simple, but cell phones can create complex family connections. That's what happened in my house when my younger children (the 'tweens) started to lobby for cell phones. Here's a rundown of their arguments:

The Whine: "But Mom, almost all my friends have cell phones...."

The It's-for-You-Pitch: "You can reach me at any time...."

The Safety or Go-for-Mom's-Heart-Pitch: "I need a cell phone just in case of an emergency...."

Giving a cell phone to a child represents a mixed connection, according to my informal poll of parents. On the positive note, cell phones enable parents to keep tabs on their kids. Cell phones also provide a channel for parents to respond to emergencies, distress or other problems children face. Additionally, many parents use cell phones to navigate through car pool delays and other transportation issues. However, there are financial questions to resolve, according to Penny McCrea, a reporter with *The Miami Herald's* Action Line consumer team.

A mother of two, McCrea has had to replace lost cell phones for her teen and college-age children. However, McCrea considers herself lucky. The lost cell phones were ultimately recovered with no fraudulent charges.

"But if the phones had gotten into the wrong hands, it would have been extremely expensive," McCrea said. "You are liable for the bill until you report the phone is missing."

As an Action Line reporter, McCrea has seen cases in which thieves have rung up thousands of dollars in international calls before the phone was reported missing.

"It's in the nature of children to lose things and to forget to tell parents," McCrea said.

In many situations, pre-paid phone plans, which place a limit on service, may provide a safeguard for parents concerned about theft and fraud. But some parents have other concerns.

"First of all, I have questions about the health risk. I assumed the risk for myself, but I'm not sure that I want to take that risk for my daughter," said one father of a 22-month-old girl.

The data from the Food and Drug Administration leaves a lot of room for parental discretion.

"The available scientific evidence does not show that any health problems are associated with using wireless phones. There is no proof, however, that wireless phones are absolutely safe," the FDA has stated.

You can minimize potential risks by limiting conversations on cell phones and using earphone devices that place a distance between your head and the cell phone, according to the FDA.

But if you want to completely avoid the possible health and financial risks associated with cell phones, you can try the "Call Home" plan my father instituted for my siblings and me during our teen years. Using a standard land-line, we had to call to report our safe arrival at a friend's house and again to announce our departure and anticipated arrival home.

One family I know maintains two cell phones, one that a parent keeps and a second one used for children during slumber parties or extended stays away from home. Upon returning home, the child surrenders the cell phone and returns to basic phone service.

My older son received his cell phone as a coming-of-age agreement. About six months after his Bar Mitzvah (age 13), he received a cell phone. He's been very responsible with it and has even used the date book feature to track school assignments. But I still think 13 is young for a cell phone. Maybe I'm just too old-school. There are even kids in first, second, and third grades with their own phones.

I was curious about what other parents do about cell phones and kids.So I delegated my parenting chores to fellow personal finance bloggers, including the crew at *www.pfblogs.org*, a site that collects daily posts from hundreds of bloggers. My mini-poll consisted of three questions and brought responses from several bloggers:

1. When do you think kids should have their own cell phone?

2. Do you make them pay for it? How do you work the finances?

3. What are your ground rules about usage and responsibility?

I received great responses from fellow bloggers.

Single Ma of Fabulous Financials, *www.fabulousfinancials.com*

1. Most kids, around age 13, begin to go places with their friends (movies, skating, bowling, the mall, etc.) and have very little adult supervision. Because of this, I gave my daughter a cell phone at 13 so I could be in contact with her at ALL times. Plus, being a single mom and living in an area with no immediate family, this was important to me.

2. Adding a second line cost me an extra $9.99 per month. I pay for the basic service but she pays for extra things (text messages, ring tones, wallpaper, new face plate, belt clip) that I don't consider a necessity.

3. As long as she doesn't exceed the shared minutes I've allotted to her, I'm ok. Whenever she does, it's taken away for leisurely purposes and used for emergencies only. She's overstepped her boundaries twice

in the past six months, so we're on an indefinite "emergency-only" basis.

Michelle of Diary of a Mad Asian Woman, *www.mishl982.blogspot.com*

"I think it's smart for kids to get a pay-as-you-go phone. Then they can realize how much they are really using the phone and how costly it can be. When they pay for it themselves, they know not to blow all their minutes and to only use it when it is important or an emergency."

Dawn of Frugal for Life, *http://frugalforlife.com*

1. "Age depends. Some 18-year-olds are less responsible than 13-year-olds."

2. "Make them pay for it or at least half if they don't have a job."

3. "Pay as you go is the best deal; that way they keep track of the time they have left."

Lazy Man and Money, *www.lazymanandmoney.com*

"I believe in starting them out early with a cell phone as long as it has GPS tracking for safety reasons. That far outweighs a lot of the other considerations, in my opinion."

Blunt Money, *www.bluntmoney.com*

"You lose it, you buy another one. Don't go over your minutes or text messages. Turn it off while in class. Keep the charger away from the pets, and unplug it when not in use."

What I learned from John Travolta's childhood

A DIY backyard pool, a bargain-basement nightclub and used designer clothes were part of John Travolta's childhood. As one of six kids, Travolta was raised by a store-owning dad and a money-saving, drama-teaching mom, who inspired John Travolta's passion for acting. I learned a lot about frugal living and parenting by reading an article about Travolta's childhood in an old issue of *Reader's Digest*.

Family backyard projects. According to the *Reader's Digest* article, the Travolta backyard was filled with DIY projects, including a fence, a large above-ground pool and a barbecue pit.

"A new pool in those days cost about $500; with a filter, it would be an $800 proposition. Instead, we got a used pool where the liner was $70 and the outside $50," John Travolta told the magazine. "My parents never limited their thinking."

Family DIY projects add a lot to family bank and memory accounts. In my house, we've had fun making birthday cards, gifts, and games with my kids. It's not really about the money; it's about the process of teaching kids to be creative and resourceful.

The secondhand wardrobe. Travolta's mom once dressed him in a used Christian Dior suit, purchased for $10 at a church thrift sale, with a retail value of about $300.

"All my clothes were beautiful, because they were the wealthy people's hand-me-downs. My mother was a smart woman," John Travolta told the magazine.

The right hand-me-downs can leave a big impact on kids. Like Travolta's mom, I also dress my kids in beautiful secondhand clothes from wealthy friends. (The grandparents also help with the wardrobe.) I also recommend shopping in thrift stores that are near or in upscale neighborhoods. Those stores often have new or only-worn-once children's clothes.

Besides, after the first washing, new, almost new, and secondhand clothes all look the same anyway. ᴾᴰ

Married with Children in South Beach

Part 2: Frugal Fun

You don't need a lot of bells and whistles to make your kids happy. If you've been a parent for any length of time, you know that. And it doesn't require a natural disaster to reveal that truth.

But after days and weeks in the dark after a hurricane knocked out power in our area, some parents walked away from the experience with this lesson: There are tons of no-cost and low-cost activities for families, ranging from "old-school" classics to high-tech battery-operated gadgets to art projects with simple crayons and watercolors.

When a blackout rolled through South Florida, simple activities—ball-games and tag-you're-it—provided exercise and entertainment.

I learned more about frugal entertainment for children during the summer of 2007, when I interviewed Chris Gardner, author of *The Pursuit of Happyness*. He also was an associate producer of the movie, starring Will Smith, which was inspired by the book.

Chris Gardner's story has been well documented. Homeless with a young child, Gardner worked as a stock broker trainee during the day. Gardner and his young child navigated through the maze of homelessness in America during nights and weekends. Ultimately, he scored big time on Wall Street and became the founder and CEO of Gardner Rich & Company, a successful brokerage firm.

When he was homeless, Chris Gardner found creative toys for his son. For example, an empty juice can made a wonderful kick-it toy.

"We'd find things," Gardner told me. "The juice container became a little soccer ball. We could make fun out of anything."

During the long stretches of weekend hours, the father-and-son team were often on the streets for extended periods. Therefore, Gardner became a pro at hunting down free community activities that kept his son entertained without spending money. Going to the park was one of their favorite activities.

Celebrity magazine pictures of Ben Affleck and Jennifer Garner with their daughter Violet on a swing set at a Vancouver playground reminded me about the backyard fun I enjoyed as a kid. While it's fun to take the kids to big-ticket, multi-media indoor playgrounds for toddlers and teens, the Ben Affleck-Jennifer Garner model of frugal fun reminds me kids just want to be active—and it really doesn't matter if it costs anything or not.

10 Fun and Cheap Activities with Kids

1. Go for a walk.

2. Play tag.

3. Make greeting cards.

4. Play board games.

5. Cook, bake and blend.

6. Call friends and relatives.

7. Draw, color and sketch.

8. Kickball, Dodge Ball and Hide-n-Seek.

9. Write letters.

10. Gardening.

Family Game Nights

Kids love board games, puzzles, charades, and action figures (my personal favorites).

Classic board games such as Monopoly, Clue, and Scrabble are available from a wide range of sources. Thrift stores, yard sales, and flea markets often sell popular games for $1 or less. Vendors on eBay also market games at low prices. And major retail chains periodically sell low-tech/no-tech games at steep discounts. I have spotted two-for-one specials and three-for-$10 game promotions at major toy chains.

Don't worry if your existing game pile is disorganized, with missing instructions and game pieces. (Mine is—isn't everyone's?) Major manufacturers such as Hasbro—maker of Yahtzee, Sorry! Life and Boggle—are happy to fill in the blanks.

Using the Internet, it's possible to download missing game instructions by logging onto the "Family Game Night" section of Hasbro's website (*www.hasbro.com*). The Family Game Night section and other parenting sites also offer great tips for setting up weekly game nights that promote quality time with family and friends.

Hasbro and other manufacturers also maintain an inventory of missing game pieces. Order forms are available online. While shopping at national toy chains, I have also spotted low-cost bags of random game pieces (dice, markers, and other common game tokens). Or you can combine secondhand games to create a complete box set. At affordable prices, Ping-Pong tables, air hockey game sets, and indoor basketball courts are sold used at thrift stores, or new sets are often sold at a discount at sports and toy stores.

The no Xbox generation

As children during the mid-1960s, my siblings and I did not need a lot to keep us happy. We did not have the electronic bells and whistles of the Xbox and our play stations included painted whistles, stones, chalk, jump ropes, and jacks.

I loved the sidewalk games: Red Light, Green Light; Mother May I; and, of course, Double Dutch.

When we jumped Double Dutch, my friends and I chanted songs while our feet hopped, danced, turned, and crisscrossed in the space between two rubber-coated jump ropes that slapped the sidewalk in syncopation.

> *"Three-six-nine.*
> *The goose drank wine*
> *The monkey chewed tobacco*
> *On the street car line.*
> *The line broke,*
> *The monkey got choke,*
> *And they all went to heaven*
> *In an old row boat.*
> *Clap, clap."*

And so, the sidewalks were heaven, especially when we had blueberry, lemon-lime, or cherry water ices dripping down our chins in the summer.

Taking lessons from those examples of no-cost, low-cost activities for kids—including my own childhood summers—I put together a list of fun, but frugal alternatives for those moments when my elementary-age daughter cries, "Mommy, I'm bored!"

25 Frugal Summer Activities for Kids

1. Write a book. My daughter Yael has written a how-to-manual for kids. It's a short guide about fixing everyday problems. She has typed up the book, and I want her to create pictures. Meanwhile, a close friend suggests another parent-child writing project: *Mommy, I'm Bored!*

2. Crafts at the library. In addition to story hour, one of our local branches offers free craft activities. My daughter made a bookmark and decorated a small wooden box.

3. Dissect old machinery. With tools and light supervision, my daughter and a friend spent hours investigating the guts of an old machine. They learned a lot and enjoyed the process.

4. Start a reading club (with other children).

5. Go to the beach, the playground or a park.

6. Check out free programs at public buildings, museums, and malls.

7. Visit botanical gardens. We found a $5 yoga class and low-cost art instructions at one of the local (public) gardens.

8. Play Neopets. There are lots of games and money-related activities at Neopets.com. Yael has actually learned a lot about commerce from *www.neopets.com*. Kids adopt electronic pets and then are responsible for feeding, housing, and entertaining their pets. Kids can play games, set up a store, and earn electronic income to support the Internet pet. I like to play the slot machines in the game arcade. It's a frugal way to gamble. I get the thrill of the casino without the expense.

9. Go for a walk.

10. Cook.

11. Shop for food. Before one grocery trip, my daughter enjoyed putting together her wish list: ice cream, berries, whipping cream, and cookie crisp cereal. Once at the store, we had fun shopping.

12. Write a letter. Yael has written cute, cute letters to my folks.

13. Start a craft project at home.

14. Go to a yard sale, flea market, or estate sale.

15. Surf the Internet for vacation ideas.

16. Look for old-school games on the Internet. My daughter googled "marbles" and found a lot of marble games. She and a friend printed out the instructions and played marbles.

17. Watch Disney Online. That's *www.Disney.com*. Also try *www.Cray ola.com* and *www.Familyfun.com*. Those websites have a variety of activities and crafts for children.

18. Free movie camps. Basically, many of the major movie theater chains have free summer movie hours for families.

19. Create a "summer buddy program." My daughter calls around looking for play dates and friends to share in new activities.

20. Co-worker program. I gave my daughter an assignment to interview my parents about how they paid for college expenses. It was a win-win-win. I really needed the information; she got to be a reporter and the grandparents were happy to chat with her. (She enjoyed herself also.)

21. Rent movies from the library. The children's selection of our local library is great.

22. Start a parent-child summer book club. I am reading the same book as my 12-year-old son. We've had some insightful short chats over food and treats.

23. Find them a job. For one afternoon, my daughter worked as a mother's helper for a friend who had an active toddler. My friend was able to finish a project, and my daughter had an afternoon of fun while playing with a toddler. She also earned a few dollars.

24. Make a list of summer activities. "Wow, I have done a lot," my daughter said as we worked on this list together.

25. Get ice cream. It's fun; it's cheap. It's cool.

Low-cost family activities

During the mid-1960s, ice cream—10 cents for a single scoop and 15 cents for a double—was one of my favorite summer treats. In the fall, we purchased red candied apples (10 cents) that stuck to our fingers. In September and October, when it was just beginning to get really cold, the sidewalks were filled with tall piles of orange, yellow, and red autumn leaves. We jumped into the leaves with our feet to the ground and our faces to the sky.

Family history was on my side as I enjoyed the streets of Philadelphia as a child. When they were children, my mother and uncle had walked four miles on Saturday mornings to attend free art classes at the Philadelphia Art Museum. Decades later, as a mom and a writer, I have followed in their footsteps and have used my phone, feet, and keyboard to find low-cost programs for my family.

From tutoring services to Internet access, public libraries offer a wealth of free programs. With a library card you can rent movies, CDs, and DVDs for free. The branch near my home has an ample supply of movies for children, tweens, and teens. My sons and daughter are happy with the selection and their contentment means that we spend less at the video store.

As a source of entertainment, libraries provide a long list of cultural programs, lectures and performances. I've spotted free music classes, and bike and backpack safety courses for school-age children. Other activities include storytelling sessions for toddlers—complete with songs, stories, finger play, and crafts. Other free programs include "Live Homework Help," in which students (fourth grade through 12) receive free and individualized tutoring in science, math, English, and social studies. The pool of tutors includes college professors, graduate students, and certified teachers. Each public library has its own menu of community programs. The free services are worth checking out.

Other no-cost or low-cost community activities for kids include city and county day camps. I've found well-run community camps for $37.50 per week, including some camps that are free or offer scholarships. My daughter has attended an excellent drama camp called the Playground Theater. The camp organizers have a generous scholarship program. What's more, many municipalities also offer specialty camps in sports, art, and education, with field trips, games, and swimming.

Unplugging the family

Once a week, as part of our Sabbath observance, my family unplugs. That translates into a world without movies, the Internet, video games or phones. It's a great way to save money, but more important, it's an opportunity to get reacquainted as a family. Our weekly disconnect yields a household of fun generated by books, conversation, and board games. What's more, my children have come to appreciate the pleasures of long walks and leisurely meals.

We're not alone. When given the choice of spending money at a mall or spending time with their parents, 57 percent of children chose more time with M&D, according to a 2003 survey conducted by the Center for a New American Dream.

"What American kids really want is not more stuff, but more time with friends and family," report the experts at New American Dream.

"Time starvation" has become a major issue for families, according to the survey results:

♦ Only 32 percent of the kids surveyed reported spending plenty of time with their parents.

♦ If they could change one aspect about their parents' work, 63 percent would cut working hours to provide more family time.

♦ Just 13 percent of kids surveyed wanted their parents to earn higher salaries.

Fortunately, there are a number of low-cost or no-cost activities that will enable you to spend more time with your children, according to the creative team from *Yes, You Can . . . Afford to Raise a Family.* Created by Sam Goller and illustrated by Paul Coker, Jr., the text offers a full menu of activities. Here are a few that I have tested with my children.

1. Detective walks. With your eyes to the ground, you and your child can scan the neighborhood for interesting items. Pretty rocks, colorful leaves and other artifacts are great for collections and conversations. My elementary-school-age daughter, for example, loves to make pretty collages from fallen leaves. For cleanliness sake, take along baby wipes.

2. Kitchen fun. My middle son is a spice king. He loves to whip up soups, cookies, and other kitchen specialties with either parent. Bonding over a battery of spices and sugar sweetens our lives.

3. Read together. Sharing a magazine is a great way to get on the same page with pre-teens and teenagers. With our oldest son, my husband and I enjoy reading the latest issue of *Game Informer*, a glossy magazine that features reviews and articles about the latest video games. This activity keeps us up-to-date on our son's interests and keeps us informed about the content of various games. In this fashion, we have an opportunity to discuss which games are suitable and which should be avoided.

Cheap Home Entertainment

There are many strategies for limiting or controlling television viewing time. One busy mom with several small children has solved her video conflicts by enrolling in Netflix, a publicly traded company that operates an online DVD movie rental service. Her plan—one of several subscription plans offered by the company—works like this: For a monthly fee, my friend receives an unlimited supply of DVDs, with no additional charges for shipping or late fees. Monthly fees range from $5.99 to $17.99, depending on your selection of options.

"Netflix is cheaper than cable. And it doesn't allow the kids access to all the cable channels," she said. "We can pick the kids' movies that we want for them."

How I get cable shows for free

In my home, we are unplugged from traditional network and cable TV, but I've found a limited way to watch some of our favorite news and sports shows without paying more or exposing the kids to an overdose of standard television.

Background: In my home, the television sets are basically monitors for DVDs and videos that we get from the library or rentals.

Problem: Occasionally, my children miss TV—which they view only at their friends' homes or when we're on vacation. I miss sports. I've become a major sports fan and I would love to watch the NBA Direct channel, NFL direct, or ESPN.

Solution: My kids like the Disney channel and we've found a frugal way to watch some of their favorite shows. Through the Internet, *www.Disney.com* lets you download and watch (almost) the complete lineup of shows, including *Hannah Montana, That's So Raven, Kim Pos-*

sible, *The Suite Life of Zack and Cody*, and other programs. A limited number of episodes are available for each show, but the rotation is current and updated regularly.

Likewise, through *www.NBA.com*, I watch highlights of all of my favorite NBA games, plus the pre-game and post-game interviews with coaches and stars. This website also had great clips of the 10 best plays of the week. The menu also includes the NBA weekly wrap-up, which is a full length talk show, analysis, and highlight program. At *www.CBS.com*, there are several full-length shows that you can watch for free. The menu includes: *CSI Miami, CSI NY, How I Met Your Mother* and *Survivor*. There are other options, including the *CBS Evening News*.

At *www.ABC.com*, I've watched *Dancing with the Stars* and *Ugly Betty*. Shows viewed on the Internet feature a minimal amount of commercials and fewer pitches, which sharply reduces viewing time. For instance, a 30-minute show is only about 22 minutes without the extended commercial breaks that are common on standard broadcasts.

How to lower cable bills

Many consumers are big fans of cable television, including Bette, a woman I know who had a monthly cable bill of $125. To my cable-free vision, Bette's expense seemed excessive. But one consumer's luxury may seem frugal to another.

"Paying for good things on your screen is actually a great use of entertainment money," wrote a fellow named Alberen. "What else can you do all day, every day all month and only spend $80 bucks on it?"

He has a point. Trips to the movies, malls, and bowling alleys can easily exceed $80 during a month's time, Alberen said. Bette believes that her cable reduces her entertainment expenses at other outlets. Consider the numbers: Weekly movie dates for two adults cost roughly $20 a week, before gas, popcorn and other expenses. On a monthly basis, four movie dates would cost at least $80. Therefore, on an hourly basis, cable is a better value, Bette said.

Even so, there are ways to squeeze more out of your cable bill, according to Melissa Tosetti, editor and publisher of *Budget Savvy*, a California-based publication now available free at *www.budgetsavvy*

mag.com. During a recent telephone interview, Tosetti, a cable fan, offered these tips:

Do your homework. At least twice a year, preferably quarterly, you should review your cable bills and check out prices offered by competing cable companies.

Think satellite. Even if your cable operator has a monopoly in your region, various satellite companies have competitive introductory promotions. Take notes.

Call the "Cancel Service Department" within your cable company, and give them details about lower prices or discounts you've found elsewhere. Be honest and be prepared with actual names and numbers, Tosetti said. It won't pay to lie.

Be persistent. Don't accept "no" on the first phone call. Repeat calls may yield a customer representative or manager more receptive to your comparison shopping. Plus, companies periodically run special promotions.

Bundle it up. Consider packaged deals that include Internet and cable access. Shop around and compare costs.

And finally, know yourself. Tosetti and her husband love the History Channel and HBO but have little use for premium sports channels. Therefore, she tailors and reduces her cable expenditures to match her tastes. Launch your own television audit to eliminate cable waste.

"Of course, don't pay for what you don't use. And watch out, the small screen is an incubator for body rot," wrote Alberen.

Manic Mom

In addition to television, sports, and camps, birthday parties are also an important part of childhood. To celebrate birthdays, we have had pirate, super hero, alien, and Pokemon parties. My husband and I have enjoyed planning birthday parties with our kids. But even with input from the kids and my husband, during family birthday parties I often morph into Ms. Manic Mom—my alter-ego. Pumped with a maternal cocktail of adrenaline and anxiety, I dash around with a single question: "Are they having fun yet?!?"

I worry about the activities, the party favors, and the atmosphere of our high-energy, but low-budget parties. It doesn't matter that we typically receive rave reviews. In Manic Mom mode, I never stop worrying.

I'm not alone. As a nation, we spend a fortune on petting zoos, bounce houses, and other party festivities for our children. We spend huge sums of cash to create a few smiles during birthday parties.

As a grandmother and veteran of many fun, but frugal, parties, Sheelagh Manheim, co-author of *Yes, You Can ... Find More Meaning in Your Life*, provided me with a few tips—especially the keep-it-simple approach.

During our interview, Manheim recalled dozens of celebrations that have generated happy memories for her children and their friends. Her kids and their guests still talk about the low-cost gypsy party in which Manheim dressed up as a fortune-teller and offered words of advice. Her basic party recipe includes a short roster of games and activities, cake-cutting ceremonies, and sweet goodbyes. And she recommends a two-hour party limit, especially for the five-and-under crowd.

Simple ball games

Here's the logic: Children are "over-programmed" during their daily lives. Play dates, homework, lessons, and other after-school activities leave little time for basic fun. Therefore, many kids particularly appreciate simple ball games and bean bag tosses. Other party favorites include craft activities in which kids make place mats or other useful items.

For a birthday party for my daughter, we purchased wooden door paddles on clearance from a national craft chain. Each package contained six wooden door paddles in different colors and sold for the discounted price of $2 a package. That's about 33 cents per favor. We also picked up discounted glitter paint, stickers, and other items to decorate the wooden door signs.

Shaped like the classic do-not-disturb hotel signs, the wooden paddles were perfect for paint, sparkles, stickers, and other tools of creativity. The kids decorated their paddles with names, initials, welcome signs or words of warning. This activity consumed a large block of time and was a hit with the boys and girls. What's more, each kid left with a practical, but unusual party favor for their bedrooms. The alternative—party bags stuffed with plastic trinkets and rubberized toys—waste money and create clutter.

"Their self-esteem comes from saying, 'I did it myself,'" Manheim said.

Donkey tails

Even Pin-the-Tail-on-the-Donkey—an old school classic—can be transformed into an exercise in self-esteem and creativity.

"We discovered that lesson by accident. As our party guests decorated their door paddles, my artistic husband quickly sketched out a donkey for the next activity. Fascinated by his artistic production, the kids drifted away from their own art projects to watch. We could have taken it a step further by letting the kids draw the donkey and create the tails," Manheim said.

"It's hysterical fun," she said about the entire process. "What matters is that they are using their imagination and doing something new."

The creator of Baby Cheapskate (*www.babycheapskate.blogspot. com*), another blogging mom, agrees with the DIY approach. Right before her son's first birthday, she and her husband received a glossy party-planning publication, featuring: "100 pages of licensed characters and every bit of cheap plastic crap you can think of to go along with them. My husband and I, both the artsy/craftsy type, got a good kick out of it. It's so much more fun to do it yourself," Baby Cheapskate noted in a written comment on my blog.

My Top 10 Tips for a Great Slumber Party

Maybe we're crazy, but my husband and I let 20 third-grade girls move into our house for an overnight slumber party. We have a family tradition of throwing sleepover parties for my children when they reach their tweens (ages 8 to 12). We spend lots of energy on these parties, but very little money. The best part of these sleepovers? My children and their classmates have a great time. Here's what we did for our daughter's party:

1. Watch a movie. Pick out a parent-approved, kid-friendly movie from either the library or the rental store. Or show a movie from your own collection. We saved money by showing a 1995 film (*Babe*) that we already owned. The girls were reading *Charlotte's Web* in school and *Babe*—a movie about a pig—was a big hit at the party.

2. Play Bingo. The kids enjoyed rounds of Bingo. We had a spirited competition, with the girls picking and calling out the numbers. We offered small prizes for winners.

3. Low-cost arts and craft projects. We took digital photos of the girls, then downloaded and printed out the photos. Using low-cost art supplies from a craft store, the girls made and decorated picture frames. Our party goers enjoyed every step of the process, especially the picture posing phase.

4. Let them bake the cake. Pushed for time, we didn't bake the birthday cake in advance. Instead, measuring, mixing, and baking became a party activity that the girls enjoyed.

5. Offer live entertainment. On the gated roof of our apartment building, my husband offered a mini-fireworks show with the girls at a safe distance. They enjoyed the color and smoke. This activity worked because we followed all safety procedures, with lots of adult supervision. Other options: a talent show, improv drama production, dance class, or magic show. Pick a showcase that relates to your in-house talents.

6. Do yoga. A few meditative poses and stretches were great for chilling out a room full of high-energy and party-happy girls. They thought it was fun and I pretended to be a yoga teacher.

7. Skip the pizza and serve pasta. It would have cost over $75 to serve pizza and fries to over 20 girls on a Saturday night. Our homemade baked ziti and fries cost less than $7 for the entire party. And the girls loved the food. We had a plain-pasta option for those who were allergic to dairy products or were picky eaters.

8. Keep breakfast simple. We just served cereal and milk. At another sleepover, we offered strawberries, waffles, and whipped cream for breakfast.

9. Curtail party hours. Our guests arrived Saturday evening, with a

"Sunday at 11 a.m." pickup time. By ending the party before lunch, we limited the amount of meals that we had to serve. We were tapped out after serving Saturday dinner and Sunday breakfast.

10. Constant adult supervision. For safety and security, my husband and I have a rule. One of us stays awake until the last child is asleep. And one of us gets up when the first child wakes up. My husband took the late shift and I woke up around 6:30 a.m. when the first kid was up. We didn't get much sleep, but we felt secure about the safety of our guests.

Masquerades and money

Americans now spend over $3 billion on Halloween, including $1.16 billion in candy, $1.15 billion in costumes, and $840 million in decorations, according to the National Retail Federation.

But you don't have to spend a lot to have fun. That's the word from Jill Cooper, a thrifty grandmother, and Tawra Kellam, her daughter. For the last eight years, the mother-and-daughter team have operated *www.livingonadime.com*, based on their book of the same title.

Cooper has fond memories of fun, but frugal, Halloween parties and costumes. As an adult, her 33-year-old son created an unusual Superman costume from his own wardrobe. Instead of buying or renting an expensive red-and-blue caped outfit, he attended a Halloween party as Clark Kent. His attire featured a standard business suit with a Superman T-shirt underneath.

"It didn't cost him anything, but we were laughing at him the whole evening," Cooper said.

She's also created her own standout costumes. She went to one party dressed in red cardboard lips, a red mask, and a Hershey Kiss apron. With bold lipstick imprints all over her face, Cooper introduced herself as the "Kissing Monster."

"I handed out Hershey Kisses all evening," she said, adding that everyone was impressed.

Cooper buys Halloween decorations at post-holiday clearance sales. She has found fake cobwebs to drape all over the party room for 25 cents a bag and orange electric lights for $1 a strand in November.

Fun, inexpensive Halloween party treats

Orange slime. Take orange gelatin and dump it onto a tray before the mix completely gels. Refrigerate and serve the slime at the party.

Floating eyeballs. Put grapes in the punch to create the illusion of floating eyes.

Bloody eyeballs. Boil cherry or grape tomatoes for half a minute. Let the tomatoes cool, then peel and serve.

Cooper and Kellam have tons of clever ideas for parties, holidays, and celebrations at their website, *www.livingonadime.com.* FD

The Driveway and the Car-Phobic Mom

There's ample parking at my Dream House, which has large driveways on opposite ends of the property—one near the northern end of the walled garden and a second on the southern corner—just below the maid's entrance. At least three cars can comfortably park in each driveway.

If I lived at the Mediterranean, I would convert one of the driveways into a mini-basketball court for my kids. Quite frankly, I don't understand the American love affair with cars; but then again, I have major issues with driving. I don't drive.

I've always been terrified of cars. As a child, I often prayed while in the back seat of the family car, even with my dad (Mr. Safety) behind the wheel. I cut simple deals with G-d. Get us there safely and I'll keep my room clean—or something like that. Later as a teenager, I sat at the curb while each of my friends earned their driver's license. But I was willing to provide safety tips from the passenger's seat as friends chauffeured me to student government meetings, football games, and parties.

While working in Pittsburgh, I finally pulled into the driver's lane at age 22. But several things undermined my roadway confidence.

First, at the Department of Motor Vehicles, my tester confessed that he should really fail me, but he charitably granted me a license anyway. I drove away feeling like a fraud.

Next, I noticed that when I drove on highways, my passengers wore roller-coaster expressions of terror and thrill. I felt like a public menace. And finally, I was banned from using the television news cars after I left the windows down during a snowstorm. Clearly, I was clueless about cars.

My mother thinks that I moved to Manhattan—with its 24/7 network of subways, buses, and cabs—in order to avoid driving. And she's right. I loved the freedom of New York's congested streets, and I was secretly relieved when my Pennsylvania license was stolen, along with my designer purse, shortly after I had relocated to New York.

Now in Miami, we have one family car, an ancient minivan, and my husband drives it. Saving money by driving older cars is a frugal strategy used by many millionaires and even a few celebrities. Teri Hatcher, co-star of the hit television show "*Desperate Housewives*" prefers to drive older cars.

"I'm a very conservative person. I drive my cars for 10 years until they have 100,000 miles on them. To me, feeling comfortable means having way more than I need in the bank," she told a reporter in the special issue of *People Extra* magazine.

One of my favorite bloggers sold her car in order to cut expenses. I received this note from Sally, a blogger at Through a Glass Darkly.

"In our march onward out of debt, Dan and I are selling my 2003 Saturn Ion 3. We never drive more than one car at a time now that we live in Midtown Atlanta, so it doesn't make sense to keep both of our cars. My car works and looks great, so I would never consider selling it if we weren't serious about dumping our debt. (I'm so sad, but it is for the best.)"

Six Keys to a Car-Free Life and $10,000 a Year in Savings

Between gas, repairs, insurance, and miscellaneous expenses, the average American pays about 18 percent of their annual income on cars, according to a 2003 survey from the U.S. Bureau of Labor Statistics.

I suspect that the 18 percent figure is actually a low-ball estimate because a gallon of gas cost only $1.55 when that survey was conducted. A 2004 American Automobile Association Study places annual average auto expenses at $8,410 or $700 a month. Of course, a car-free life is not for everyone. But it's possible to save $5,000 to $10,000 each year by letting go of your car, or cutting back to one car in your household.

There are six key questions to ask yourself, if you're thinking of living a car-free life according to Chris Balish, author of *How To Live Well Without Owning a Car.*

1. *Can you put the brakes on your ego?* Balish makes a valid point. If you don't drive a car, many people think you are a loser. That attitude has been partially fed by the automobile industry, which has done a lot to promote the connection between wheels, financial status, and self worth.

And indeed, while I have waited at bus stops, I have received expressions of pity and sympathy from motorists. I've learned to bypass the pity factor. I like the freedom to read and write during my commute.

2. *Is it possible for you to commute to work without a car?* I've used public transportation, cabs, and carpools.

3. *Is your home in an urban area or a mixed-used development community?*

4. *Do you have easy access to public transportation?*

5. *Do you live close to shopping districts, entertainment establishments, banks, and other basic life services?*

6. *How flexible is your schedule?*

Traveling on Big Wheels

Many consumers have reservations about public transportation. Complaints range from schedules, convenience, and access. Many of those concerns are valid, but as gas prices climb, buses, and trains provide affordable and energy-efficient options.

There are also fare discount programs for individuals, senior citizens, veterans, and students. Many transit programs also offer group discount plans for companies. But even without discounts, buses, subways, trolleys, and trains represent a good bargain. It's a frugal way to travel.

Tips for public transportation travel

1. Check the schedule. Buses and trains run frequently in New York, London, and Boston. But in other major metropolitan areas, including Miami, it's best to review the schedule before leaving your home. Schedules are often posted online and many transportation systems have free trip planning services that provide schedule and route information over the phone.

2. Carry exact fare amounts. Most bus operators don't offer change, and it's annoying and wasteful to pay $2 for a $1.50 fare.

3. Ask about discounts. Most municipalities offer weekly or monthly passes, special promotions, and assorted discount programs.

4. Leave time for potential delays. Traffic jams happen.

5. Bring a book, magazine, school work, or office assignments. Riding a bus is like traveling in a long stretch limo. Sit in the back and do your work, while the uniformed chauffeur drives you around. Use cell phones discreetly and leave your laptop in the bag. Keep track of your packages.

My Scooter, Costco and Gas Savings

To function in Miami without a driver's license, I've adopted several strategies, including mastery of a scooter. I thought I was cool. On the foot-pedaled Razor scooter (a secondhand Sharper Image toy), I ran errands, checked in on my kids during their school day, and squeezed in a bit of exercise while saving money on gas.

But I had second thoughts about my fuel-saving push when I looked at the bemused expressions on the faces of my kids. They seemed embarrassed, and I suspected that I had jumped from the cool-mom category into the weird-lady column. I deciphered the code of playground politics. Other moms drive sensible minivans or SUVs. But the Rosenberg mom pushes a little scooter. Mindful of appearances, I put away my thrift-mobile.

I realized to be really serious about saving gas, there were many other options. I didn't need a Razor scooter to be fuel efficient. I get lifts from road-weary friends and cab drivers, and I walk a lot. Additionally, I help my husband (our family driver) track down the cheapest prices for gas. From unusual fuel vendors to price-checking services, it's possible to contain gas costs even during the peak summer travel months.

From your home computer, you can track the lowest gas prices. *www.GasPriceWatch.com* and *www.GasBuddy.com* are two of the Internet-based sites that provide gas prices based on zip code, city, state, and region. By providing a zip code, you can locate the lowest prices within a region or neighborhood.

During a casual conversation, a friend mentioned that she was going to Costco, one of several wholesale clubs in the nation. And although her shopping list included such standard items as bulk purchases of paper goods and tuna fish, she also had plans to fill up her tank at Costco.

I made a few phone calls and I discovered that Costco sells gas at about two-thirds of its 238 warehouse stores in the United States. And the prices tend to be lower than local gas stations.

"That's our goal. We want to offer the lowest prices in the warehouse and at the gas stations," said Bob Nelson, a spokesman for Costco told me. There is one catch. You have to be a member of Costco to gas up at the store's pump. But often pump savings outweigh the $50 cost of the annual club membership, according to Gas Buddy.

Other wholesale outlets such as BJ's Wholesale Club and Sam's Club also sells gas at various stores. BJ's spokesperson Sharyn Frankel said, "Prices are typically four to six cents less than the average price in the market."

At Sam's Club, company spokesman Olan James declined to give specific numbers, but said, "We try to be competitive in the markets where we sell gas."

For many retailers, low gas prices are a loss leader—a lure—to get you into the store, where higher-profit items are for sale, according to GasBuddy. Meanwhile, beware of service stations that are annexed to auto repair shops. Gas is typically higher at those outlets.

Carpooling

When I first arrived in Miami, I worked downtown. I gratefully car-pooled with Michael Cole, a Miami Beach neighbor and co-worker. The arrangement saved time, money, and fuel. What's more, as Michael drove over the Julia Tuttle Causeway, we had ample time to discuss work projects and neighborhood events. A friendship developed between our two families.

The benefits of carpooling are many, especially as the combined punch of national tragedies, world economies and fuel shortages have hiked the price of fuel. A number of national and regional programs help commuters find carpool partners. And the numbers of carpoolers have dramatically increased, according to Steven Schoeffler, executive director of *www.eRideShare.com*, an Internet-based bulletin board for commuters.

"The impact of gasoline prices on ride-sharing from my perspective is unmistakable, and I've seen increases reported by other ride-sharing organizations also," Schoeffler told me.

Consider the numbers. The American Automobile Association estimates that it costs an average of 54.1 cents a mile to operate a car, based on mid-year prices. At that rate, a 40-mile round-trip trek to work would cost $21.64.

"People are realizing that they can save thousands of dollars a year by carpooling," Schoeffler said. "At the same time, they know they're helping to reduce our dependence on foreign oil and reducing green-house gas emission by sharing the ride."

Cheapest cars to insure

We recently shaved $1,000 a year from our auto insurance bill by switching from a well-known auto insurer to Geico, *www.Geico.com*. I recently interviewed an insurance agent, who stressed the importance of comparing auto rates. He estimates that consumers could save a couple hundred dollars per quarterly period by rate shopping. He deals with nearly every insurer in the business and has spotted big differences in rates for comparable cars in the same region. Bottom line, it pays to shop your auto insurance.

Valet parking nightmares

In addition to car insurance, parking can be another nightmare for drivers. On that subject, I've learned lots from Kenneth, a family friend who has a lot to say about valet parking. He'd rather walk a few blocks to a park-it-yourself meter than hand over his car keys to a valet parking employee. His fear is based on experience; Kenneth has either witnessed or heard tales about valet parkers who scratch, dent, or otherwise damage automobiles in their care.

"They abuse the cars," he said. "The more expensive the car, the more open it is for abuse."

Frankly, I used to politely smile whenever Kenneth offered one of his tirades on parking. And then it happened. In 2005, my husband and I attended back-to-back parties on the same night. After the first party, we blissfully drove away in our humble red Dodge Caravan, after tipping the valet parker, who closed our car doors for us.

Our trouble began just minutes later at our next stop, when my husband tried to open his door on the driver's side. The inside door handle, which worked fine before we handed it over to the first valet parker, was jammed. In a hurry to hop from party to party, we had not noticed the damage until it was too late.

But Kenneth has a solution.

193

"When the valet parker gives you your car, do a quick once-over to make sure everything is OK," Kenneth said. "If you do see a scratch or dent that wasn't there before, report it immediately."

He quickly concedes that not all valet parkers mishandle cars and, in fact, there are many responsible valet parkers out there. In addition, valet parkers can be a friendly source of inside tips about sightseeing, dining, and even parking.

My newspaper editor, for example, received a valuable tip from a valet parker at one of the oceanfront hotels in Miami Beach, where a community-awards banquet was being held. The valet kindly pointed my editor to a large public lot, where parking was significantly cheaper.

Nevertheless, Kenneth prefers to park his own cars at conferences, parties, and other large events. "It's worth walking a few blocks to save time, aggravation, and money," Kenneth said.

Walking Tours

With the year-round supply of warm days and ocean breezes, Miami is an ideal setting for a walker like me.

I became a serious walker during my years in New York. From the Upper West Side to Lower Manhattan, I loved to walk all over New York. Like my grandmother Julia, I could walk for hours and I enjoyed taking out-of-town visitors on extensive walking tours. For instance, when my great aunts—Julia's sisters—came to visit me from Philadelphia, I gave them a walking tour of Midtown Manhattan, the Theater District and the Village.

"She's just like her grandmother," I overheard my Aunt Vera tell my Aunt Liza. "Yes. Indeed," Aunt Liza said. "She's the walkingest child."

Walking is one of the cheapest, easiest, and healthiest forms of exercise. I walk about one mile daily, sometimes more.

10 reasons why I enjoy walking

    1. *I don't need to buy fancy or expensive equipment.* (I buy great athletic shoes on sale. My Reeboks, for example, were purchased at a BOGO-half off sale at Macy's.)

2. *No gym needed.*

3. *Walking fits into small time slots of the day.*

4. *I can walk and accomplish other tasks and errands.* The post office is a half-mile from my home. Buying stamps is an easy way to log in a mile.

5. *Walking is meditative.*

6. *Walking is the cheapest form of transportation.*

7. *A stroll is good for the heart and easy on the joints.*

8. *I can walk alone or in groups.*

9. *It's a fun exercise to do with kids.*

10. *I don't need to enroll in a class, watch a tape, or hire a personal trainer.*

"You don't have to join a gym," Dr. Arthur Agatston, author of *The South Beach Diet*, once told me when I was researching an article about fitness. "Too many people will get excited and join a gym for a month and then just stop."

During our phone interview, Agatston prescribed a simple program for fitness. A brisk 20- to 30-minute walk, undertaken three to five times a week, can yield strong health benefits, Agatston said. Health benefits can also be achieved in shorter spurts, according to the Centers for Disease Control and Prevention (CDC), a federal agency based in Atlanta. For example, if you live or work in a tall building, try taking the stairs instead of the elevator.

"Using the stairs requires little or no additional time, no wardrobe change, and no additional cost," the CDC writes in its publication "*StairWELL to Better Health.*"

Even regular household chores such as gardening, mopping, and hammering can help you shed pounds, according Lowe's Companies, which operates a nationwide chain of home improvement stores. And once again, it's cheap!

To calculate the health benefits of household chores, Lowe's tapped the expertise of Liz Neporent, co-author of *Fitness for Dummies*, and author of *The Ultimate Body: Ten Perfect Workouts for Women.*

Housework and Calories

Type of Exercise	Minutes	Calories Burned	Equivalent
Raking Leaves or Washing Windows	20	3.4 per minute	30 minutes of walking
Mowing the Lawn with Push Mower	20	4.6 per minute	30 minutes of leisurely cycling
Weeding Garden or Refinishing Cabinets	40	6.9 per minute	30 miniutes weight training
Painting or Cleaning Rain Gutters	45	9 per minute	30 minutes jogging at 5 mph

Source. *Fitness for Dummies* and Lowe's

Walk to School! Save Money; Get Fit!

I also have fond memories of walking to Pennell Elementary School through thick piles of autumn leaves in Philadelphia. The route to school was well-marked and lined with uniformed crossing guards and badge-carrying members of the student safety squad.

I am reminded of those memories whenever I see the Barasch family walking to and from school on weekdays. Their daily drill is an exercise in saving money, gas, and health, said Stuart Barasch, a lawyer and father of students of Mollie and Jacob.

Unfortunately, the once-popular stroll to school is a rare event for most families. Due to safety concerns and time constraints very few students walk to school. In fact, the Centers for Disease Control and Prevention (the CDC) estimates that walking or biking trips account for only 15 percent of student commutes.

However, due to the double threat of childhood obesity and rising gas prices, some parents are re-thinking the car pool. (Not only have gas prices spiked far above $3.00 per gallon, but the percentage of overweight children has tripled over the last 30 years.)

As an alternative, the "Walking School Bus," has become a popular pedestrian vehicle in some communities. Government agencies, non-profit groups, and informal networks of parents are re-claiming the streets through "Walking School Bus" campaigns.

A walking school bus works just like a car pool, and consists of "a group of children walking to school with one or more adults," according to the Pedestrian and Bicycle Information Center at the University of North Carolina Highway Safety Research Center—one of several organizations that promotes walking school bus programs in the United States.

At a very basic level, a walking bus or bike pool involves two families, with adults assigned to different days. On a more involved level, ambitious groups establish an elaborate system of structured routes, meeting points, volunteers, and timetables. But regardless of the structure, adult participation and supervision are the keys to the car-less car pool.

The CDC recommends a ratio of one adult participant for every six children aboard the walking bus, with an option of fewer adults for students age 10 and up. However, for children ages four to six, experts recommend a one-to-three ratio.

Of course, walking your child to school requires time and organization. But busy parents can carve out the extra time. Consider that once or twice a week a walking bus workout can take the place of a gym circuit or a tennis match.

And if your family lives too far to walk, consider a partial workout. Park your car at a healthy distance from school, and then walk the remaining blocks. Keep in mind that walking will also help you skip past lengthy and time-consuming carpool lanes at school. Take baby steps. Begin with a limited walking schedule of once a week or even once a month. But above all, have fun.

Time spent walking with your children (and their friends) is valuable. I've had the opportunity to walk with my older sons and I have really enjoyed their company. Walking is good for the heart, and we're saving on gas. PD

My Home is a Zoo

How many pets can we squeeze into a three-bedroom apartment? Quite a bit if you ask my children. Our household proves that you can live in an apartment and still have a zoo. We own one dog and have had at one time two medium-sized turtles, three hermit crabs, one frog, several hamsters, a rabbit, a few snails, and several goldfish.

I can only imagine how many pets we would own if we lived in my Dream House, with its huge backyard, frog pond, and gardens. With our zoo, the Dream House would probably resemble a Dream Shelter for animals.

We weren't always a pet-friendly family. In fact, we opened our doors to animals only after years of avoiding the high-pitched pet pleas from our kids. Based on our experience, I have two bits of advice for parents of pet-craving children, especially when it comes to a dog.

First. Realize that it's your pet, not the kids. Most children lose a bit of interest after the second week. And even if they don't, kids have play dates, parties, and after-school activities. Kids go away to camp or off to college. And during those long blocks of time, the adults in the home will spend many hours alone with the family pet. Therefore, as a responsible adult, you will walk, train, feed, and play with the dog most of the time. What's more, most likely you will fall in love with the dog.

Second. Pets are a great learning and parenting tool. In all fairness, our kids do pitch in to help with our dog, Scruffy. Not as much as we imagined, but there is a sense of shared responsibility and commitment. We've all become more disciplined.

Scruffy, Our Life and Money Coach

Our pets aren't normal animals. And Scruffy, the latest addition to our home, is more than just a dog. Scruffy is our lifestyle guru—with wise lessons on money management, organization, and recycling. Our lessons begin every morning around 6:45 when our teacher—Scruffy— barks his first command. Get up and take me out! Life with Scruffy has been a life-altering experience.

Since adopting Scruffy from a private animal rescue program, our home life has jumped to the next level in terms of planning, spending, and saving. The choice was simple. We could either be overrun by our dog, or we could pick up our pace.

Here is a quick overview of the lessons I've learned about adopting a pet and dealing with a puppy.

Ask questions, get specific answers. We adopted Scruffy from a wonderful organization that was passionately devoted to Scruffy and his five siblings. The dogs were abandoned in a bag in front of a supermarket when they were just weeks old.

Pet rescue organizations are a great source. Pet adoption organizations are a great way to adopt pets. Naively, my family assumed that the adoption was a free or minimal-fee service. However, on the day that we picked up our dog we faced a surprise bill of $200 for the adoption, medical shots, and other services. The fee was reasonable considering what the vet bills might have been. But if we had asked more questions from the outset, writing the check would have been easier.

Recycle. Forget the expensive pooper scoopers and other gadgets. Plastic bags are great for protecting your hands while cleaning up after a pet. It's a great use for discarded bags. Old tennis balls and puppy-friendly stuffed animals can be rejuvenated as great chew toys for dogs. Scruffy even likes to play paw-ball with empty plastic bottles.

Guard your valuables. Shoes, eyeglasses, and books are expensive chew toys. Through costly missteps, my family—especially the kids—has learned painful lessons about disorganization. My daughter brought a chewed-up homework assignment to show her grade-school teacher. "The dog really did eat my homework," my daughter said.

Consider dollar stores. My husband has found some wonderful pet items at a dollar store. We even found a red-dot laser tag game for Scruffy for one buck, down from $7-$10 at a local pet boutique.

Know your limits. We purchased clippers for Scruffy's long dark nails. But after one unsuccessful nail-trimming attempt, we decided to pay the dog groomer for that service. (We found a $5 puppy pedicure deal.) No harm was done to the puppy. But clipping his nails was too painful for us.

Finally, the biggest lesson involves organization. Scruffy is at his best when we provide a well-structured day, with clearly-defined times for meals, walks and play. Our puppy is a great teacher.

Woman Unleashed:
Five fiscal lessons from my dog

I've covered Wall Street for years, but I received new financial lessons from Scruffy.

1. Get a grip

Scenario. As I walk my dog, I am pulled in different directions because I have yet to develop a firm command. It's not a pretty picture. Scruffy has even escaped from the leash when I've totally lost control.

Lesson. Likewise, when shopping I often feel pulled in different directions. And through many trials and lots of errors, I've learned the value of shopping with a list and a fixed agenda.

Shopping with a defined purpose—as opposed to recreational browsing—enables me to get a better grip on my cash, the checkbook and the debit card. I also track the charges on statements and receipts for mistakes, gaps, and leaks. Without control, I'll be chasing tails and running into unfriendly traffic.

2. Prepare for rain and storms

Scenario. My dog does not like going outside to do "his business" in the rain and thunder.

Lesson. Learn to operate under difficult conditions. Always, always have a Plan B or an exit strategy for businesses and investments. For Scruffy, we developed an alternate route. There is a covered outdoor path and grassy patch under our apartment building. It's near the trash room, protected and perfect for rainy days.

3. Clean up the mess

Scenario. As a dog owner, I deal with a lot of waste, especially when my dog rips up newspapers around the house. To maintain order, we have to constantly be neat and tidy.

Lesson. Fiscal and physical tidiness are constant efforts. It's just a fact of life. Stay organized and armed with a pooper scooper.

4. Create long-term plans

Scenario. Vacations, out-of-town visits and even day trips are a challenge with a new puppy. It's difficult to find hotels and friends that are hospitable to pets. It's expensive to find doggy daycare.

Lesson. My failure to plan is not someone else's emergency. That means saving for major vacations and making early reservations for the best travel rates. And of course, we have to make boarding arrangements for Scruffy in advance. Failure to plan ahead, I've learned, creates unnecessary expenses and anxiety.

5. Get educated

Scenario. My puppy—so adorable—jumps on the dining room table and jumps on guests. It's time for more puppy training.

Lesson. Ignorance and lack of training are not excuses. Likewise, for my fiscal education, there are many free and affordable resources. The Humane Society and various animal shelters have affordable puppy training classes. There are online resources and books in the library.

Poor Mario: A Hamster's Obit and My Lost Money

In addition to Scruffy there have been other members of our pet family—Mario was one of those members. Toward the end of his short life, Mario developed tumors. In a frantic attempt to save his life (and my children's hearts), my husband and I visited two animal specialists. We spent about $250 in medical bills for our beloved Mario, a $6 hamster from the pet store.

We could have saved a lot of heartache and dollars, if we had done our homework. Hamsters—as we later discovered—have short lives and tumors are a sign of the end. Our misdirected kindness only prolonged Mario's pain and cost us a fortune.

Frugal warnings from pet specialists

Careful research is the ticket for pet care, according to the experts at animal shelters, who offer a long list of tips for pet owners. From warnings about unscrupulous breeders to low-cost health care for pets, local not-for-profit animal rescue operations have a wide range of free resources for pet-loving households.

Bad breeders. The problems that face would-be pet owners are numerous. For instance, due to an unscrupulous puppy breeder, Lee—a savvy insurance broker—spent over $1,500 on a Teacup Yorkie puppy that died quickly after the sale. Within three days, the puppy became sick and Lee spent an additional $430 dollars in emergency vet care. The animal died within days and Lee later discovered that the animal breeder had a bad reputation for running a "puppy mill," that peddles problem or sick animals to the public.

Puppy mills. Puppy mills are breeding operations where animals are housed in crowded quarters, with minimal care. Purebred puppies born in such overcrowded conditions often develop illnesses or behavior problems, according to animal experts.

Therefore, it's important to investigate a private breeder's background and business. Many breeders run excellent operations, but some unsavory characters prey on pet-loving families.

In Lee's case, the breeder refused to reimburse him for the cost of the sick puppy. But backed by a state Lemon Law for cars, which also applies to puppies, Lee is taking the breeder to small claims court. In the future, he plans to carefully research the history and the reputation of other breeders before making a purchase.

Costly designer mutts. Unscrupulous breeders are also selling mixed-breed dogs with cute names and high prices ($1,000 and up), according to Cherie Wachter, director of Marketing for the Humane Society of Broward County, Florida. These so-called novelty dogs include. "Labradoodles," a cross between a Labrador and a Poodle, and "Schnoodles," a mix of a Schnauzer and a Poodle.

"Buyer beware," Wachter said. "Basically what you have is a mixed-breed—a mutt. There are plenty of mutts at shelters all over the country."

Mutts and pure-bred animals are available at low costs. For instance, the Humane Society of Greater Miami offers pets at a rate of $60 for cats, and $90 for dogs, according to Melanie Otero, public relations director for the non-profit organiztion.

Likewise, the Humane Society of Broward County charges $70 for cats, $85 for dogs, and $95 for puppies. Both agencies provide a wide range of health, indentification, and support services with each pet adoption.

"We have a wonderful selection of dogs and cats of every breed, size, color, and shape imaginable," a spokesman from one agency told me.

Pure-breds for less. And surprisingly, many non-profit agencies have pure-bred animals for adoption that would cost at least $500 to $1,000 or more in the private market. My friend Lisa adopted her Flame Point Himalayan cat from a local branch of the Humane Society. FD

Hurricanes, Brushfires, and Other Financial Storms

L ife in South Beach is great. I live in a postcard of sun, ocean breezes, palm trees, and sand. But there is a major downside to life in paradise—namely unwelcome guests like Wilma, Andrew, and Ivan. Hurricanes, tropical storms, and tornadoes have destroyed lives and homes in South Florida.

Hurricane season lasts from June 1 to November 1, according to Frank Lepore, public affairs officer for the National Weather Center.

Unfortunately, Lepore said, too many residents postpone hurricane preparations until lines for seasonal merchandise are long and prices are very high. Consumers should purchase canned goods, water, batteries, and other hurricane-related supplies before the stores are swamped with panic buyers.

"Each family and each business needs to have a plan for what they're going to do," Lepore told me during an interview.

Other areas of the country are also hit by floods, earthquakes, wildfires, and tornadoes. You don't have to live in Florida to maintain a stock of emergency supplies. For example, I once read about a California man who drives around with a 72-hour emergency supply kit in his car. But beyond the safety issue, there's frugal sense in early preparation, according to the folks at the National Weather Center.

A shop–now strategy enables you to take advantage of sales and weekly specials offered by different retailers. Items like water, batteries, and nonperishable lunch treats are frequently sold at sharp discounts.

Emergency List

1. Buy bottled water when it's on sale and save it! (Water that is more than a year old can be used to flush toilets when water becomes a scarce commodity.) Collect clean containers, thermoses and water coolers. Fill empty vessels (gallons and gallons) with enough water for your household. This is not excessive. During Hurricane Wilma in 2005, we lost water for almost two days. We valued every drop in our stockpile.

2. Fill the tub if your local forecast includes a hurricane, a major electric storm, or tornado. (Ignore this advice, or lock the bathroom door if you have small children in the house.) When we lost our running water during Wilma, I was so glad we had filled up the bathtub. That water was used to flush the toilet and wash hands.

3. Keep soapless hand sanitizers and baby wipes around.

4. Buy batteries on sale. Almost every week, Walgreens, CVS, Target, Rite Aid, and other national chains offer batteries on sale. Keep an alphabet of battery-operated electricity. Buy up paper plates and plastic cutlery. Those items are important if you don't have electricity or water.

5. Set up a supply drawer and don't borrow from the stash. If you use emergency supplies for leisure activities, you won't have necessities during emergencies. Stock the drawer or shelf with batteries, flashlights, candles, matches, canned goods, nuts, and other non-perishables. Keep a supply of books-on-tape, flashlights, paper goods, fun snacks, instant soups, and camp cooking supplies. These items are so helpful in a power outage or during a post-storm period of disarray. It's also important to have an emergency stash of cash. When the power goes out, credit cards, ATM machines and electronic debit cards are useless.

6. And though it sounds weird, set up a "safe room" in your home. For us that means a window-less area where we can retreat when high winds are an unwelcome guest in paradise.

An Evacuation Kit for Your Money

I've spent a lot of time compiling a three-day emergency kit—water, canned goods, batteries—for my home. But what about a backup plan for our money? Financial professionals argue that we should take the same precautions for our finances as we do our homes.

Pre-Emergency preps

Establish a secure store of important financial data.

♦ List of your banks and other institutions. Keep a list of financial institutions, including banks, credit unions, credit card companies, and other lenders. Store the list in a secure place and omit account numbers.

♦ List of branch office locations. If you are planning to evacuate make sure to get a list of the branch offices and affiliates of your branch in other markets. This information is usually available online.

♦ Backup and store your information. Use a safe deposit box to keep backup copies of key documents. Information can be stored on a CD or a flash drive that is locked into a vault.

♦ Your phone list. Maintain a list of key phone numbers: relatives, employers, utility companies (water, electric, landline, cell phone, cable, and Internet), insurance companies (health, auto, and home), mortgage lenders, doctors, landlord, lawyer, accountant, home repair company, and investment professionals.

Evacuation Carry-on Luggage: Data for your travels

♦ Home inventory. A list of your possessions, especially valuables. Photos of the inside and outside of your home. Take digital photos that can be emailed and later retrieved. "Before-pictures" (pre-damage photographs) are important for filing insurance claims in the event of extensive damage due to fire, water, or wind.

♦ Cash is king. Small bills and even coins are valuable during emergencies.

♦ Documents. Bring along pay stubs and recent tax documents. This information may be necessary if you have to apply for an emergency loan or credit line while evacuated, according to Bank of America.

Freezers and Blackouts

During storm-prone months, many consumers deliberately reduce the load on the family freezer because of the fear of power loss. But I have chatted with two appliance experts about freezers and power outages. Representatives from both companies touted the benefits of a packed freezer during a power outage.

"Generally speaking a full freezer is going to retain cold longer, with food items serving as blocks of ice that help maintain sub-zero temperatures longer," according to an email reply from Stacie Barnett, a spokeswoman for Sub-Zero Freezer Company.

Dean Schwartz, a refrigerator buyer for Sears Holding Corp. (Kenmore appliances), agrees. A packed freezer, Schwartz said, has fewer pockets of warm air.

"Keep it shut," he said. "Humidity is a huge enemy of a freezer or a refrigerator."

Both companies declined to comment on how long food is safe after a power outage.

"Because of so many environmental factors, we don't note a maximum length of time that food is safe after a power outage. Rather, Sub-Zero advises homeowners to know the "danger zone" for unsafe food temperature. Generally, food spoilage occurs between 40 to 140 degrees Fahrenheit," Barnett wrote in her email. "Therefore, in the event of a power outage, it is advised that consumers stick a thermometer in the freezer to assess the temperature. Keeping the door closed keeps food colder longer, but check the thermometer occasionally to assess when the "danger zone" is reached. Homeowners never want to leave food in the danger zone for more than two hours."

One blogger, Adrift At Sea added this bit of freezer advice.

"Another good thing to do is to leave a pile of ice cubes in a ziplock bag, inside the freezer. Then if you open the freezer after a power outage, or when you return from a vacation, check the ziplock bag. If the bag has a solid block of ice in the bottom, it means that the freezer was off for long enough for the ice cubes to melt, and that all of the food in it is suspect."

A sense of community

My neighbors are a blessing. When our town was hit with a series of storms—especially Hurricane Wilma—my apartment building neighbors provided a bedrock of comfort. It was a community effort in saving dollars, sense, and sanity.

Without water or electricity, we took turns wearing various hats—chef, baby-sitter, librarian, shopper, custodian, and designated driver. Through our combined efforts, we've given new meaning to the phrase "retail chain." With various links from apartment to apartment, our building served as a freestanding mall of services and goods.

Babysitting. With a large number of kids in our building, child-care duties were shared through a traveling play group. Armed with puzzles, books, blocks, and battery-operated trinkets, parents and older children took turns watching younger children in different apartments. This cooperative enabled parents to unwind, make repairs, and work without worrying about the safety and care of small children.

Professional shopper. Neighbors en route to stores took orders from others. For instance, when my friend Tracy was planning a trip to a local supermarket, she dropped off her young boys in our apartment and picked up our shopping list.

Free bed-and-breakfast inn. After basic utilities were restored to our neighborhood, many people in my building opened their two- and three-bedroom apartments to friends and families from nearby towns that lacked power, water, or other basic services. One weekend, for example, my sister-in-law, her husband and two kids (who had no electricity after a hurricane) stayed with us.

Our neighbors down the hall provided refuge for their son, daughter-in-law, and their children. What's more, the daughter-in-law's parents also moved into the apartment for the weekend. All told, there were three families, representing three generations, in one apartment.

Librarians. Puzzles, games, books, and magazines have been traded among neighbors. My younger son and daughter even swapped Game-Boy cartridges with new friends.

Catering services. When the power was out, food was often shared and distributed. For example, as her frozen milk and ice cream defrosted, one neighbor distributed cartons of milk to others. She had far more than she could use by the hurricane-accelerated expiration date. My husband Avi and I supplied a grill and gas, while several neighbors offered a wide menu of goodies. Leftovers were shared with others.

Outlet shopping. Batteries, foil pans, CD/radio/tape players, baby wipes, celery, Disney movies, shoes, and children's clothing were among the items exchanged among neighbors and friends.

Not all the help came from those within the building. Neighbors, friends, and family from other parts of the city and state offered assistance. What's more, through the collection of money, clothing, food, and other supplies, we've also donated and helped areas of Lousiana, Texas, and other storm-hit regions of the country. Clearly, a lot of goodwill and gratitude circulate with the high winds during our season of unwelcome guests.

The Earthquake and the Talking Dog

An earthquake hit the Florida-Louisiana region one Sunday morning in 2006. I thought I was crazy, but I learned a few frugal lessons.

Scenario: 11 am Sunday; Miami Beach. I was on the couch. It's a heavy piece of furniture, but it moved. Initially, I thought that I was experiencing the side effects of a sugar-caffeine overload. But no, the world moved. I felt caught in the 1999 hit movie, *The Matrix* because physical reality had shifted.

Me:	The couch is moving!
Hubby:	Someone's kicking the couch.
Me:	No! The couch is really shaking.
Daughter:	And the dog is talking.
Everyone:	Laughter.

I was amused by my daughter's wit. My kids are funny. But about ten minutes later, my news-savvy parents call from Central Florida with a bulletin about an earthquake in Florida, a rare event. I related my experience and I felt validated.

Here's what I learned from the earthquake.

1. *Trust your gut.* Like Neo, the reality-defying action-hero from *The Matrix*, I felt a glitch in time and space. It was real. But too often, I've made silly financial or professional decisions because I've denied gut feelings about glitches in products, services, or events.

2. *Little things matter.* The couch did not move a lot, but my world view was definitely altered. Small movements can count a lot. Sometimes, in a push to achieve slam-dunk/big-ticket/fill-in-the cliché success, I ignore the "loose change" or the minor gains and focus just on the major savings. But honestly, nickel-and-dime moments in savings, debt reduction, and career growth can add up to major shifts in lifestyle.

3. *Talking dog moments.* A sense of humor is worth a large fortune. ᴾᴰ

211

How Jennifer Lopez and Ben Affleck Saved Me

A fully functional, wood-burning fireplace seems odd in tropical Miami, but that bright red fireplace in my Dream House represents a practical fixture in a Depression-Era structure.

Built before the days of central air and heating systems, the Mediterranean's fireplace was designed to provide warmth during Miami winters.

From November through March, Miami typically has about 40 days of chilly—and at times downright cold—weather. On those days, a fireplace makes sense and whenever I see that structure, I feel instantly comforted and transported back to the Northeast winters of my childhood.

The family room of my parents' suburban Dream House also had a large brick fireplace. Almost every fall my father had our chimney cleaned, and he arranged for a delivery of wood to feed the flames. Near the fireplace, my father had a black reclining chair with a footrest that flipped forward when the chair rocked back. We all loved sitting in that chair, especially when our poodle Josie cuddled next to us.

Once, maybe late summer or early fall, my Dad sat in that chair and talked about his life. Presenting a quick sketch of the difficulties and the parental desertions that both he and my mom had faced, my father said that he and my mom had tried to give their children as much as possible, including the emotional and material benefits that were absent from their Depression-Era childhood. He hoped, therefore, that I would give my children even more. I nodded, and it felt like a promise.

No Dream House

Several decades and thousands of miles later, the Mediterranean's red fireplace reminds me of that promise. But I fear that I have not fully upheld my end of the bargain. You see, my parents raised a family in a split-level, suburban home with a wide back porch overlooking a small hill lined with tall evergreens. My children are growing up in a three-bedroom apartment with a small balcony.

Although the balcony looks out onto an expansive and expensive view of the Atlantic Ocean, including palm trees, million dollar homes, and glitzy buildings, it is still a small balcony in a modest apartment. Bottom line, I do not live in a Dream House.

It's tempting to blame my housing woes on the runaway South Beach real estate market of the new millennium and the deplorable lack of affordable housing in many communities. And I have met other young professionals—smart and seemingly savvy about money—who sing the same sad tale. Over lunch, one of my former business editors griped about the spike in real estate prices. She and her husband—transplants from the Midwest—experienced sticker shock during their first encounter with Florida real estate prices. The so-called starter homes she toured ranged from $300,000 to $400,000, and that was years ago.

"Now there's no hope," the editor said, referring to prices of $800,000 and up in desirable neighborhoods.

Her story is my story. But there's a sub-plot that I must own up to. I have made personal, financial, and professional choices that have landed me on a seventh-floor balcony.

For example, about two years before the terrorist attacks of September 11, my husband and I toured the Humble House, a two-bedroom, two-bath home that lacked central air conditioning and other perks. The garage—the agent argued—could be converted into a third bedroom. And the price was right at about $200,000.

I sniffed.

"My apartment is bigger than this house," I complained.

In less than 10 years, the Humble House has spiked to almost a million dollars. Subsequent owners have installed a central air and heating system and have converted the garage into a large bedroom. The neighbor next door does seems to be disturbed—patrolling the street with rants and violent threats. And in fact, one afternoon his bizarre behavior even prompted me to change my walking route. "We're so lucky we didn't buy that house," I tell myself over and over. But I'm not so sure.

Homeownership moved further away, shortly after September 11, when I left my job as a well-paid business reporter for the *Daily Business Review*. I traded the comfort of a fixed salary and benefits to pursue my dream of becoming a mainstream newspaper columnist and a freelance writer. With assignments from the *Miami Herald*, *People* magazine and other publications, I launched a new stage of my career.

But in moments of doubt, I fear that I have traded a Dream House—complete with a backyard and front lawn for my kids—for personal glory.

Maybe, I argue, I should have kept the steady paycheck, purchased the Humble House and told my kids to just avoid the Crazy Man Next Door. Or I could have flipped the Humble House—sold it for a tidy profit—and used the money to buy my Dream House.

My younger siblings purchased their dream homes the old-fashioned way. They saved. After graduating from the University of Pittsburgh, for example, my sister Debra married and purchased a home in a suburban community in western Pennsylvania. With lush mountains and a new base of high-tech industry, the Pittsburgh metropolitan area remains a very affordable region, with attractive and luxurious homes at reasonable prices.

But more than geographical luck contributed to me sister's home ownership. "I opened up a savings account and I put $200 a month into it. I put my birthday and Christmas money into it. I cashed in some stock options. And then I put myself on a budget," Debra said.

The Harvey Siblings' Home-Buying Guide

♦ Bring lunch from home; eliminate take-out or restaurant lunches.

♦ Locate first-time, home-buying programs. Debra attained an affordable mortgage by attending weekly home-buying classes for first-time house hunters.

♦ Examine a wide number of homes. Debra toured 57 homes before selecting the right property.

♦ Check your credit report, recommends my brother Ben. After requesting a copy of his report, he corrected errors and repaired negative comments by contacting lenders and creditors.

♦ Hide your ATM card. While saving for a home, Ben often left his ATM card at home in order to avoid impulse purchases. He also created a 20-percent savings tax. For every dollar he spent, he placed 20 percent of the purchase price into the bank.

♦ Use investment profits. After posting sharp gains in the securities market, my siblings used a portion of their Wall Street profits to finance Main Street property dreams.

♦ Create an emergency house fund. Buying the home is only part of the picture. Just ask my sister Karen. Shortly after she purchased her Central Florida home, the structure was battered by 22 hours of 80-mile-an-hour winds during a hurricane. "Water came straight though," my sister recalls. Even with insurance coverage, my sister had to pay $3,000 for repairs. Her advice to would-be homeowners: "Be prepared for unexpected expenses and emergencies."

Meanwhile, in my rental apartment, the should-haves, would-haves, and could-haves dance in my head with the steady beat of a Hip-Hop music video. And doubt flickers like strobe lights in a trendy South Beach club.

JLo and Ben to the rescue

During those grim moments of doubt, Jennifer Lopez and Ben Affleck save me. In a weird sort of way, I feel as if know them quite well. That's because I was part of the army of photographers and reporters who parked in front Jennifer Lopez's Miami Beach waterfront mansion when her engagement to Ben Affleck crumpled into "Bennifer" tabloid head-lines.

Professionally, I sort of stalked Jennifer Lopez—known as JLo at the time. I tracked her trail through grocery stores, South Beach stores, a Regal Cinema, and a beauty salon—the headquarters of a celebrity styl-ist who created many of the updos, bouffant flips, and other hair fash-ions that she has sported on the red carpet.

I earned that plum assignment because my apartment building was within blocks of the waterfront mansion Lopez owned at the time. On the clock, I sat at her curbside for hours and recorded the corporate names and license plate numbers of her landscape crew, pool service team, and caterer. When I was tracking her she was hot news and a photograph of her was worth a large fortune.

Lopez was hiding and I actually felt sorry for her. I had seen my own life crumple after a broken engagement. But during my meltdown, I had the luxury of privacy. Sure, my family, co-workers, and roommates knew of my troubles and self-inflicted problems, but to the cashier at the Greek coffee shop in Midtown Manhattan, I was just another spoiled urban professional waiting for a latte. I melted into the crowd like sugar in coffee.

But Lopez was a hot news story and a prisoner in her own home. Re-portedly, she even hid in the back of a service truck to sneak away to a clandestine reunion with Ben Affleck during the height of the uproar.

I may have pitied her, but I sat on that curb in front of her house earning an hourly fee and picking up hot tips from her neighbors. It was rumored that when Lopez wanted to go out jogging, she ran at bizarre hours—after midnight with body guards—reported one of her neighbors as I wrote down his comments. Who needs a mansion, I wondered, if it's just a fancy cage? Scribbling in my reporter's notepad, I recorded key lessons about the perks of privacy.

As a reporter, I've interviewed homeless people, victims of crime, and mothers in soup lines. Motivated by guilt and goodwill, I've donated money and materials to those hard hit by hurricanes and other misfortunes. In our small global news village, it's hard to feel untouched by the tragedy of others. But over the click of cameras and the buzz of helicopters, Jennifer Lopez and Ben Affleck spoke to me in parental tones. *Be grateful for your life and good fortune.*

Surprisingly, Jennifer Lopez schooled me well on the art of frugal living. She downsized her life by ditching the big mansion, with the round-the-clock army of security guards, and elaborate pool and house parties. She married singer Marc Anthony and launched a seemingly quieter chapter in her life.

Lopez has moved out of my "hood," out of Miami and out of the Southeast. I've lost track of her, but I often wonder if her new view is as nice as mine.

Meanwhile, whenever I want to see my Dream House, I can just look out the window or stand on my "porch." Sometimes, when I walk the dog, I'm tempted to open the garden gate and step into the large lush lawn. But that's trespassing and I feel oddly protective of the house. I have even picked up trash—water bottles and paper cups—from a nearby sidewalk. And I feel very annoyed when the garden crew fails to make a regular visit and the lawn appears unkempt and untidy. Always the reporter, I want to write down the corporate name of the garden team and report the crew's negligence to the real estate agent who is trying to sell my Dream House.

My kids share my Mediterranean fascination. For instance, while walking to a neighborhood park in the summer of 2007, my daughter pointed out the house to her buddies.

"We're going to buy that house," she said softly.

One of her companions—a six-year-old boy named Danny, who also lives in our apartment building—pouted when he heard news of our pending move. Our families are close. We have shared meals, sugar, and laundry detergent. My older boys have watched Danny and his siblings when their parents go out. And almost every Friday night, my daughter knocks on their door for a bowl of hot chicken soup.

As we walked away from my Dream House, my daughter noticed Danny's gloom. My children have felt the same way when long-time friends have moved out of the apartment building and into houses. I recognized that left-behind feeling on Danny's face and my stomach rumbled with unease. What sort of nonsense was I feeding my children, I wondered? Even my middle son, a junior high school student, had begun to tell people that we were going to buy a $2.6 million home.

"Don't worry," my daughter told Danny in a confidential voice that wasn't intended for my ears. "The house is a lot of money. First, my mother has to sell a lot of books; my dad has to do a lot of business, and we have to save lots of money."

I smiled. I could visit the red fireplace in the Mediterranean without guilt. My M&D could be proud of me.

No, I don't have a house, But I've given my children the family deed on dreams, frugal living, and hard work. And with those gifts, I can live comfortably on my balcony because I already have a dream home in South Beach. ᴾᴰ

Acknowledgments

I did not write this book alone. Nearly every page sports fingerprints—virtual or literal—from my friends, family, and co-workers, who have blessed my life with their wisdom, humor and love. Therefore with gratitude to Hashem, (G-d), I thank you all.

Special thanks to my parents: Barbara and Benjamin Harvey (M&D) for all of the years of generous support, love, and insight. Thanks for letting me tell stories about your house-hunting adventures. I appreciate the extensive interviews and the unconditional love. Thanks also to my siblings: Ben Harvey Jr., Karen Harvey, and Debra and Frank Patterson, who have also opened their wallets and hearts to support my literary pursuits.

I'd also like to thank my husband Avi Rosenberg, who has been my partner in frugal living and has contributed love, creativity, and good humor to this chapter of life. I could not have written this book without the love and talents of my school-age children, Tali, Gabi and Yael, who helped me to interview different family members. (Great interviews, Yael and Gabi!) Special credit to Tali Rosenberg, who gave up many pickup games of basketball to work as my unpaid research assistant during the summer of 2007. Many of the charts and facts were assembled and researched by Tali.

With gratitude I thank the following family members who provided interviews, memories or other forms of support: My in-laws: Frumma Rosenberg-Gottlieb, Yosef Rosenberg, Hindy and Rabbi Rafi Rosenberg, Gittel Lazerson, Leiba Rosenberg, Rochel and Shaul Shifrin, Shimon and Chaya Rosenberg, Tanya Rosenberg and Yigal Rosenberg.

The following relatives and close family friends graciously shared memories with me: Norma and Isaac Groom, Frank Stephens Jr., Phyliss Griffin, Elizabeth Morgan, Vera Capron, John Wardlaw, Susie Johnson, and Lenard and Bea Harvey. Special gratitude to my deceased grandmothers, who are a big part of this memoir: Julia Wardlaw Stephens and Gertrude Beatrice Harvey.

Also thanks to: Ruth and Thomas Anderson, Martha and John Jarrett, Nathalie Berry and Deborah Gilbert—a childhood friend, a former New York roommate and a great photographer. Special thanks to Harriet Brown, a poet, writer, and childhood friend.

Thanks to friends in Miami, who have provided either emotional, financial, or creative support:

Elaine Dobin, Leah Bitton, Monica Hill, David and Jill Smith, M. Gary and Melisa Neuman, Esther Neuman, Tammy and Kenny Goldring, Lydia Goldring, Nathan and Ellen (Goldberg) Katz, Deborah and Adrian Muller, Helene and Jeff Gassner, Gary and Nina Yarus, Holly and Warren Gross, Neil and Tracy Vaisleberg, Rabbi Akiva and

Chana Lee Stolper, Jay and Caroline Schechter and Rabbi Kalman and Rucha Baumann.

I also offer appreciation to RASG Hebrew Academy and Toras Emes Academy.

Thank you to Mitchell Kaplan of Books and Books in the greater Miami area. Thanks to Bob Mecoy, a wonderful agent with great insights, Donna Jarrell, The Southhampton Writers Conference, the Key West Writers Conference, and Writers @ Work.

At the *Miami Herald*: I have a special place of gratitude to my editors and friends: Kathy Foster, who edits my weekly column in the Home and Design Section of the *Miami Herald,* and to Teresa Mears, the editor who hired me to write the frugal column at the *Herald*. Thanks also to Lisa Gibbs, Brenda Krebs, John Dorschner, and Terence Shepherd from the *Miami Herald*.

Also thanks to Ed Wasserman, Jackie Bueno-Sousa, Craig Matters, and Mark Vogel.

Thanks to the Staff of DPL Press. Thank you, Cathy Hollenbeck for wonderful edits, ideas, support, and open-hearted-generosity. I also express gratitude to Mary Hunt of *Debt-Proof Living,* and Kristen Bergman for her excellent attention to this manuscript.

Thanks to friends in New York. I express gratitude to the following people in the New York area: Tom and Kathy Lamont. As editor of the newsletter division at *Institiutional Investor (II)*, Tom Lamont has been my mentor and a frugal living role model (a.k.a. "The Cheapskate"). Thanks also to David Faber, now at CNBC, and one of my editors when I was at *II*. Thanks Faber for reviewing a much earlier version of this manuscript. Thanks for telling me that my *Black Princess* novel was really awful.

Thanks also to Rabbi Meir Fund, Elizabeth Judd, Lyn Perlmuth, Mark Voorhees, and Mindy Rosenthal.

Special thanks to my editors at *Florida Trend* magazine, *People* magazine and *Money Magazine*. Thanks also to the marketing staff in the corporate office of Baptist Hospital and to the *MacNeil Lehrer Report*, (where I was an intern in the fall of 1980). Special thanks to Andrea Roane, anchorwoman in the D.C. area.

WTAE-TV in Pittsburgh: Jim Scott, Joe Rovitto, Lynn Cullen, Kerry Kelty, and Harold Hawk. Thank you to all of the photographers and reporters who helped me during my early years in Pittsburgh.

Thank you to Georgetown University and to the following professors: Dr. Roland Flint, Dr. James Slevin, Father Timothy Healy, Ph.D., and Dr. Paul Cardacci.

Thanks to all of my high school teachers at Cherry Hill High School West.

And for those that I have not thanked by name, please know that your names and images are indelibly written in my heart.

With love and gratitude,

Sharon

MORE TITLES FROM
DPL PRESS, INC.

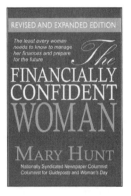

The Financially
Confident Woman
978-1-9345080-1-5

In Stores NOW
$14.95

Hired@Home
978-0-9760791-9-4

In Stores NOW!
$14.95

No Fear
Entrepreneur
978-0-9760791-6-3

Coming SOON

Tiptionary 2
978-0-9760791-5-6
In Stores NOW
$14.95

Debt-Proof
Living
978-0-9760791-1-8
In Stores NOW
$16.99

Debt-Proof Your
KIDS
978-09760791-4-9
In Stores NOW
$14.99

Available wherever fine books are sold or call 800 550-3502